# SOCIAL JUSTICE IN THE HEBREW BIBLE

# SOCIAL JUSTICE
# IN
# THE HEBREW BIBLE
## What Is New and What Is Old

*Bruce V. Malchow*

**A Michael Glazier Book**
THE LITURGICAL PRESS
Collegeville, Minnesota

A Michael Glazier Book published by The Liturgical Press

*Cover design* by David Manahan, O.S.B. "Sometimes the Blind Have Comforted Those Who See," etching. Georges Rouault, 1871–1958. Photo courtesy of St. Procopius Abbey, Lisle, Illinois.

4    5    6    7    8

**Library of Congress Cataloging-in-Publication Data**

Malchow, Bruce V., 1940–
    Social justice in the Hebrew Bible / Bruce V. Malchow.
       p.  cm.
    "A Michael Glazier book."
    Includes bibliographical references (p.   ).
    ISBN 0-8146-5523-8
    1. Social justice—Biblical teaching.  2. Bible.  O.T.—Theology.
I.  Title.
BS1199.J8M35   1996
241'.622'0901—dc20
                                   95-37823
                                      CIP

*For Tim, Laura, and Mike*

# Contents

# Abbreviations

| | |
|---|---|
| AB | Anchor Bible |
| *ABD* | David Noel Freedman, and others, eds. *The Anchor Bible Dictionary.* 6 vols. New York: Doubleday, 1992. |
| *ANET* | Pritchard, J., ed. *Ancient Near Eastern Texts Relating to the Old Testament.* 3rd ed. Princeton: Princeton University, 1969. |
| *BTB* | *Biblical Theology Bulletin* |
| BZAW | Beihefte zur Zeitschrift für die alttestamentliche Wissenschaft |
| CBC | The Cambridge Bible Commentary |
| *CBQ* | *Catholic Biblical Quarterly* |
| *CurTM* | *Currents in Theology and Mission* |
| *Exp Tim* | *Expository Times* |
| *HUCA* | *Hebrew Union College Annual* |
| *IDB* | George Buttrick, and others, eds. *The Interpreter's Dictionary of the Bible.* 4 vols. Nashville: Abingdon, 1962. |
| *IDBSupp.* | Keith Crim, and others, eds. *The Interpreter's Dictionary of the Bible.* Supplementary Volume. Nashville: Abingdon, 1976. |
| *JBC* | Raymond Brown, Joseph Fitzmyer, and Roland Murphy, eds. *The Jerome Biblical Commentary.* Englewood Cliffs: Prentice-Hall, 1968. |
| *JBL* | *Journal of Biblical Literature* |
| *JNES* | *Journal of Near Eastern Studies* |
| *JSOT* | *Journal for the Study of the Old Testament* |
| NAB | New American Bible |
| NJB | New Jerusalem Bible |

| | |
|---|---|
| NRSV | New Revised Standard Version |
| OTL | Old Testament Library |
| *RB* | *Revue biblique* |
| REB | Revised English Bible |
| RSV | Revised Standard Version |
| *TDNT* | Gerhard Kittel, and Gerhard Friedrich, eds. *Theological Dictionary of the New Testament.* 10 vols. Grand Rapids: Eerdmans, 1964–1976. |
| *TDOT* | Johannes Botterweck, and Helmer Ringgren, eds. *Theological Dictionary of the Old Testament.* 5 vols. Grand Rapids: Eerdmans, 1974–1986. |
| *VT* | *Vetus Testamentum* |
| VTS | Vetus Testamentum, Supplements |
| WMANT | Wissenschaftliche Monographien zum Alten und Neuen Testament |
| *ZAW* | *Zeitschrift für die alttestamentliche Wissenschaft* |

# Introduction

## The Current Situation

Social injustice is a major problem facing the world today. At times, the word "injustice" implies illegal acts which deprive people of their rights. However, many unjust acts in the present age are legal since the present structure of society allows them to exist. However, people with moral sensitivity recognize that these acts are inherently unfair because they place certain groups at economic or social disadvantage. Such activity prevents these people from having equal access to basic conditions for life.

First, this kind of injustice exists in the United States and other so-called First World countries. The structure of society here favors the rich and places the poor at a disadvantage. The wealthy hold political, economic, and social power, and thus, they are able to control decisions which are made in these areas. Such decisions, therefore, often benefit the rich, and inevitably, they make life harder for the poor.

For example, the rich often exert undue influence on the way tax money is spent. The poor pay as much sales tax on items bought as the wealthy. Yet, the rich have the power to insure that this tax is spent on items they want, like magnificent public buildings, rather than on programs for the poor. Also, wealthy employers hire inordinate numbers of part-time workers so that the employers do not have to give employees full-time salaries and benefits. If the poor are fortunate enough to get these jobs, they remain poor. Employers demand that middle-class employees work heavy overtime so that the employers do not have to hire additional workers. Thus, they avoid paying benefits to additional employees. In this way fewer jobs are available for the poor, and the rich grow richer.

In the United States social injustice is also often the result of racial or ethnic discrimination. African Americans, people of Mexican, Caribbean, Central and South American origin, and Native Americans are not treated as the equals of whites. Many of them are poor and seem to be trapped in perpetual poverty. In the case of the African Americans, their poverty originated in their former slavery. Few have been able to rise above their needy condition because there is so much that makes doing so extremely difficult. Their children are not properly prepared to enter school since they lack the early educational experiences that other children have. This includes simple things like looking through magazines and books and going to museums and zoos. When the children begin school, they are less ready than other children their age to learn, so school goes badly for many of them. When they finish, many are less prepared than other graduates to compete in the job market. So fewer African Americans are employed and, thus, continue to be poor and to raise children with as little chance as they had. Many wealthy and middle-class whites see little reason to do something to break this pattern since the status quo benefits them.

However, some African Americans put out the additional energy that it takes to break out of this cycle. Some become well educated, get good jobs, or start their own businesses. But it is harder for them, people of Mexican, Caribbean, Central and South American origin, and Native Americans than for others because discrimination constantly blocks their way. Whites repeatedly doubt that people in these groups know as much or can work as well as others. Some whites oppose them simply because of their color. So they are bypassed and not given a chance to prove themselves. Again, those with wealth and power keep the poor from improving their lot.

The problem in the world at large is even greater. It centers on what citizens of the United States regularly call the Third World. However, since some people in those countries consider that a pejorative term, we shall use the phrase they prefer, "developing nations." The poverty in those places is alarming. 1.2

billion people live in absolute poverty, with barely enough to sustain life. One billion, and one-third of them under age two, are malnourished. Seventy percent of deaths in developing nations each year are related to problems caused by hunger. In the forty-two poorest countries, 25 percent die before age five.

Comparison of the developing nations with the United States reveals enormous disparity. Those nations contain 76 percent of the world's population and receive only 27 percent of its income. On the other hand, the United States has only 6 percent of the earth's population but uses 40 percent of its resources. The average citizen of the United States consumes as many resources as it takes to sustain ninety people in India. The average world citizen utilizes four hundred pounds of grain a year while the average person in the United States uses a ton. Only two hundred pounds of this amount are ingested directly. Much of the rest of it is wasted because it is fed to animals which are later eaten.[2]

Social injustice is the cause of much of this disparity. Manual laborers in the developing nations prepare their national resources for export to the United States and other major powers. They receive minimal payment for their work and resources while exported items are sold at a much higher price in the importing countries. The large profits are shared by the importers in those places and by the exporters in the developing nations. The wealthy in both places grow still richer while the poor laborers in the developing nations receive little and remain poor. The elite in both places are happy to maintain the status quo. Middle-class workers in the United States and other major powers support them because these employees believe that they derive benefit from this system. However, considering the extent of poverty in the developing nations, the injustice in this system is horrendous.

### Combining Efforts

How does the Church in the United States respond to this problem? Many in the Church support this national and world social injustice because they are part of the United States' economic, political, and social system. Living in this country, much that we do without reflection adds to the problem. But when we become aware of the injustice, what can we do about it? Opposing it means opposing much of the power structure of this country. How can the comparatively small number of concerned Christians make a difference? This problem becomes more acute as the Church becomes an increasingly small percentage of the nation's population. Important decisions about social justice are made in the public arena, where decreasing numbers of Christians are present. And yet, the Church's insights into social justice need to be represented there. A single decision of Congress can affect world poverty much more than the total donations from all religious bodies and charities in an entire year.

Yet, the Church surely does not contain all citizens of the United States who are concerned about social justice. There are increasing numbers of Moslems, Jews, Buddhists, and adherents of other world religions in this country. Many of them and many non-religious people are committed to social justice. It would be extremely helpful if their efforts and Christians' efforts could be combined. That process would be accelerated if non-Christians and Christians could reach some ideological agreement on the issue of social justice. Would Christians be open to that development? How could Christians integrate the thought of these other people with their own thought on this subject?

This is by no means the first time that people in our tradition have faced this question since it was already faced by the ancient Israelites. The following chapters will demonstrate that Israel did not originate the concept of social justice. It was present in other countries of the Near East before Israel, and Israel received the legacy of their thought on the subject. However, Israel faced new situations involving justice during its history. How did it meet them? How did it integrate the legacy of Near Eastern thought on the topic with its own approaches to the new problems?

Hans Walter Wolff and Walter Brueggemann have developed a paradigm which speaks to this question. According to them, Israel's tradition grew in the following manner. At any given moment, Israel had a previous tradition of past memories of God's dealing with them. In the present Israel encountered new crises. The combination of its tradition with its thought about the new crises resulted in new affirmations of faith or new tradition. Thus, Israel's tradition was regularly reshaped and remained alive and growing. According to Wolff and Brueggemann, therefore, the primary question that we are to put to any text of the Hebrew Bible is: "What in this text can we discern of the meeting between memory and the historical pressure?"[3]

This paradigm can be applied to our question. Israel did not only receive its own tradition about God's dealings with them from the past. It also received the legacy of Near Eastern thought, and it integrated that thought with its own Yahwistic tradition in the manner which Wolff and Brueggemann have described. When Israel faced crises over justice, it combined old Near Eastern ideas about justice and its own past experience with its new thought about the subject. Out of this combination it developed a relevant approach to the new situation. Thus, Israel's justice tradition continued to grow and constantly remained relevant to the changing conditions of life.

In a different context, speaking about resources available to the Church, the Gospel of Matthew said: "Every scribe who has been trained for the kingdom of heaven is like the master of a household who brings out of his treasure what is new and what is old" (13:52). Israel's approach to social justice was also to bring out of its treasure what was new and what was old. It combined the old traditions of the Near East with its new approaches to current problems.

This book examines what the Hebrew Bible has to say about social justice. We shall watch for the ways in which Israel adapted its Near Eastern tradition to the new problems it faced. This should provide clues on how we might integrate the thought of non-Christians about social justice with our own. We are confronted with the same problem of integration that Israel was. What can Israel teach us about meeting it?

### Notes

1. Jerry Folk, *Doing Theology, Doing Justice* (Minneapolis: Fortress, 1991) 31–33.

2. Ralph Klein, "The God of the Bible Confronts the Politics of Hunger," *CurTM* 17 (1990) 112.

3. Walter Brueggemann and Hans Walter Wolff, *The Vitality of Old Testament Traditions*, 2nd ed. (Atlanta: John Knox, 1982) 11–12.

# 1

# *Origins of Israel's Concern*

The ultimate origins of Israel's concern for social justice lay in the earlier Near Eastern treatment of the issue. We shall first examine what the Near East had to say about this subject. A later origin of Israel's concern came from its own foundational experience in the Exodus. We shall look at that source later.

## *Near Eastern Concern*

Most interpreters are agreed today that Israel received its concern for social justice from the Near Eastern cultures surrounding it.[1] In fact, protection of the poor, widows, and fatherless children was a common policy in the Near East. In Mesopotamia there are frequent references to this concern as early as Sumerian times (ca. 2850-2360 B.C.E.).[2] It is mentioned in Mesopotamian legal texts like the reformatory measures of Urukagina of Lagesh and the Code of Ur-Nammu and in Wisdom writings such as the Babylonian Theodicy and the Proverbs of Utnapishtim.[3]

The care of the weak begins with the gods. A hymn to Shamash says:

> You create justice for the weak,
> give judgment to the orphan girl.
> The weak you make a hero,
> the insignificant you make rich.[4]

Monarchs, next, represent the gods in carrying out this duty. Mesopotamians believed that the gods gave divine justice to rulers.⁵ They had special responsibility to provide justice for the deprived in their role as highest judge. Lipit-Ishtar of Isin calls himself a king

> who causes the righteous to come off victorious forever,
> who speaks the word of justice in court and decision.

He says: "I have established justice for Sumer and Akkad."⁶ The prologue to the Code of Hammurabi states that the gods

> Anum and Enlil named me
> to promote the welfare of the people,
> me, Hammurabi, the devout, god-fearing prince,
> to cause justice to prevail in the land,
> to destroy the wicked and the evil.
> that the strong might not oppress the weak.⁷

In the epilogue, Hammurabi says

> I sheltered them [the peoples of the land] in my wisdom.
> In order that the strong might not oppress the weak,
> that justice might be dealt the orphan (and) the widow.⁸

Finally, the care of the weak is expanded from the ruler's duty into a responsibility for ordinary people. The Counsels of Wisdom incorporate a lofty sense of justice:

> Unto your opponent do no evil;
> Your evildoer recompense with good;
> Unto your enemy let justice [be done].⁹

This work also recommends charity for the needy:

> Give food to eat, give date wine to drink;
> The one begging for alms honor, clothe.¹⁰

Social justice was also a dominant theme in Egyptian litera- ture. It occurs in ideal biographies, declarations of innocence, in- scriptions, hymns, and Wisdom writings.¹¹ Social justice was particularly important during the First Intermediate (twenty- second to twenty-first centuries B.C.E.) and the Middle Kingdom (twenty-first to eighteenth centuries). Those with power were asked to deal impartially with all or even to seek out and meet human need. This appeal is made in several Wisdom writings of this period, such as The Protests of the Eloquent Peasant, Merikare, Amenemhet, and Ipuwer.[12] As in Mesopotamia, some of them, particularly Amenemhet and Ipuwer, stress the role of the monarch in providing justice.

However, justice was highlighted in other eras also. The gods were seen as the originators of justice, as they were in Mesopotamia. A hymn says:

> Amon, lend thine ear
> to one who is alone in the court,
> in which he is poor, he is not rich.
> When the court defrauds him of silver and gold, . . .
> May Amon transform himself
> into a vizier in order to release the poor.[13]

Also, justice was the ideal for people who were not royalty. The Inscription of Intef the herald claims that he was "free from partiality, justifying the just, . . . servant of the poor, father of fatherless, . . . protector of the weak, advocate of him who has been deprived of his possession by one stronger than he, husband of the widow."[14]

As in Mesopotamia, there were also calls for charity to the poor. An old Wisdom writing, Ptahhotep, says: "Do not be miserly with thy wealth, which has accrued to thee as the gift of god."[15] A declaration of innocence states: "I have given bread to the hungry, water to the thirsty, clothing to the naked, and a ferry-boat to him who was marooned."[16]

One Wisdom writing, the Instruction of Amenemopet, is remarkably detailed in its prescriptions for just behavior. It declares:

> Do not carry off the landmark at the boundaries of
> the arable land, . . .
> Be not greedy for the property of a poor man,
> Nor hunger for his bread. . . .
> If thou findest a large debt against a poor man,
> Make it into three parts,
> Forgive two, and let one stand. . . .
> Do not lean on the scales nor falsify the weights, . . .

> Do not accept the bribe of a powerful man,
> Nor oppress for him the disabled.[17]

There are also other occasional statements on social justice from other areas of the Near East. From the Hittites come these commands of the king to the border guards: "One should not favor a superior . . . should not take bribes . . . do whatever is right . . . if a widow has a case judge it and set it right . . . a stranger who resides in the Land provide him fully with seeds, cattle, and sheep."[18] The Phoenician Kilamuwa Inscription describes the ruler's relationship to the lowly in this way:

> But I was for one a father,
> and I was for another a mother,
> and I was for a third a brother.
> And the one who has never seen the face of a sheep
> I made the owner of a flock;
> And the one who has never seen the face of an ox
> I made the owner of a herd,
> and the owner of silver and the owner of gold.
> The one who had never seen a tunic from his youth
> in my own days was clothed with byssos.[19]

Finally, the Ugaritic texts show that Canaanite kings also were expected to judge the unprotected fairly. In the Keret text, the king is condemned for not living up to his responsibility:

> Thou judgest not the cause of the widow,
> Nor adjudicat'st the case of the wretched;
> Driv'st not out them that prey on the poor;
> Feed'st not the fatherless before thee,
> The widow behind thy back.[20]

And in Aqhat, it says of King Danel that he:

> Is upright, sitting before the gate,
> Beneath a mighty tree on the threshing floor,
> Judging the cause of the widow,
> Adjudicating the case of the fatherless.[21]

Thus, it is clear that justice for the weak was a common concern throughout the Near East long before Israel existed. Israel received this theme from the other countries. There are many concepts in the texts above which will be utilized in the biblical materials. For example, the god is the origin of the notion of justice. Then, the ruler represents the god in implementing it on earth. Finally, it becomes the responsibility of all people. Those who benefit from the display of justice are the weak, the poor, widows, fatherless children, and, in the Hittite text, the stranger.

The act which is praised most often is just judgment of the weak. This includes not being partial toward the strong and not allowing them to oppress the defenseless. Charitable gifts for the poor are also frequently commended. The Egyptian Instruction of Amenemope added several specific concerns: not moving landmarks, not seizing the property of the poor, reducing the size of their debts, not falsifying weights, and not taking bribes. The Hittite text also had the last item. All of these details will reappear when we reach the biblical texts.

## *The Exodus*

When Israel faced justice issues, it drew on earlier Near Eastern resources. It also used its own birth experience in the Exodus as a base. Israel knew well what social injustice was because it had been born in that condition. Israel came into being in a situation of oppression in Egypt. The Book of Exodus says that the Egyptians "set taskmasters over them (the Israelites) to oppress them with forced labor. They built supply cities, Pithom and Rameses, for Pharaoh. . . . The Egyptians became ruthless in imposing tasks on the Israelites, and made their lives bitter with hard service" (1:11, 13-14). The Egyptians compelled the Israelites to work at arduous tasks against their will. According to the story, the Egyptians accelerated the oppression by attempting genocide next. They tried to kill all Israelite, baby boys who were born.

And Israel suffered under its oppression. The text says: "The Israelites groaned under their slavery, and cried out. Out of the slavery their cry for help rose up to God. God heard their groaning, and God remembered his covenant with Abraham, Isaac, and Jacob. God looked upon the Israelites, and God took notice of them" (2:23-25). Israel cried out with misery and complaint, and God knew their agony. And so, God came to deliver. Yahweh was a God who cared about the pain of oppression. When the Israelites suffered it, Yahweh soon responded. God set them free from their servitude and rescued them from the tyranny of the Egyptians. And it was on the basis of this deliverance that Yahweh established a covenant with Israel. Yahweh became their God, and they became God's people.

Thus, the Exodus became the foundation of Israel's faith. It was the basis for knowing who Yahweh was and who they were. Yahweh was a God who delivered from oppression, and Israel was Yahweh's people. So Israel repeatedly used the Exodus as a foundation in its later writings. Israel evoked the memory of the Exodus in law codes (e.g., Lev 25:38; Deut 5:15), prophetic writings (Isa 63:11-14; Hos 11:1), psalms (106), and other texts. The Exodus became the model for God's willingness to save suffering people.

So when Israel faced situations of injustice, it drew its resources for meeting them from Near Eastern thought on the subject, which existed long before there was an Israel, and from the subsequent Exodus event at the beginning of its history.

●   Notes

1. F. Charles Fensham, "Widow, Orphan, and the Poor in Ancient Near Eastern Legal and Wisdom Literature," *JNES* 21 (1962) 129; H. Eberhard von Waldow, "Social Responsibility and Social Structure in Early Israel," *CBQ* 32 (1970) 184–85; Harriet Havice, "The Concern for the Widow and the Fatherless in the Ancient Near East" (Ph.D. diss., Yale University, 1979); O. S. Rankin, *Israel's Wisdom Literature* (Edinburgh: Clark, 1936) 13–15; Johannes Fichtner, *Die altorientalische Weisheit in ihrer israelitisch-jüdischen Ausprägung,* BZAW 62 (Giessen: Töpelmann, 1933) 26–31.

2. Samuel Kramer, *The Sumerians* (Chicago: University of Chicago, 1963) 264.

3. Fensham, "Widow, Orphan," 130–31.

4. Quoted in Havice, "Concern for the Widow," 150.

5. Hans-Joachim Kraus, *Psalms 60–150, A Commentary,* trans. Hilton Oswald (Minneapolis: Augsburg, 1989) 78.

6. Ibid.

7. *ANET,* 164.

8. Ibid., 178.

9. Ibid., 426.

10. Ibid.

11. Havice, "Concern for the Widow," 31–32, 47, 65–66, 75, 83–84.

12. *ANET,* 407–10, 414 19, 441–44.

13. Quoted in Havice, "Concern for the Widow," 84.

14. Ibid., 75.

15. *ANET,* 414.

16. Ibid., 36.

17. Ibid., 422–24.

18. Quoted in Moshe Weinfeld, *Deuteronomy 1–11,* AB 5 (New York: Doubleday, 1991) 439.

19. Quoted in Norman Habel, *The Book of Job, A Commentary,* OTL (Philadelphia: Westminster, 1985) 436.

20. *ANET,* 149.

21. Ibid., 151.

# 2

# Social Setting of Israel's Concern

Before examining what the Hebrew Bible has to say about social justice, we shall look at a few parts of Israel's social setting in this chapter. This survey will help to clarify the subsequent examination of Scripture.

## Class Structure

Israel's class structure changed during its history. Scholars generally agree that early Israel was not divided into classes and that there was considerable equality among Israelites. However, there is wide disagreement on why this was so. To understand this disagreement, it is necessary to look briefly at the origins of Israel.

There are, at least, four major approaches today to the question of where Israel came from. The first is the invasion model. A typical proponent of it is John Bright.[1] This model follows the portrayal of events in the Book of Joshua. According to this scheme, a united Israel invaded Canaan under the leadership of Joshua toward the end of the thirteenth century B.C.E. They first attacked the center of the country and later, the cities of the south and Hazor in the far north. They successfully conquered these places and proceeded to distribute the whole land to the various tribes of Israel.

There are major problems with this model. First, it disagrees with the first chapter of Judges, which pictures the conquest of the land as a piecemeal process conducted by individual tribes over an extended period of time. Second, it is not supported well by archaeology. Very few of the cities which the Book of Joshua says were destroyed by Israel show signs of destruction at this time. Oddly enough, other Canaanite cities were destroyed then, but there is no way of being sure who did the damage. Canaan was regularly a battleground with various nations fighting there. Consequently, the invasion model is little accepted today by critical scholars.

The second theory, which is well represented by the work of Martin Noth,[2] is the immigration model. According to it, unconnected tribes entered Canaan individually at various times from the patriarchal period to the time of David. Ultimately, these tribes became Israel. They did not destroy the previous population of Canaan and fought with them only sporadically. It was David who first conquered the Canaanites. A major problem with this model is also archaeological. One would expect significant cultural differences between sites settled by Israelites and held by Canaanites. But there is so much cultural continuity on sites in Canaan generally that there seems to be little basis for distinguishing between Israelites and Canaanites. Thus, the immigration model has little popularity today.

The problem with this immigration model leads logically to the third theory, the revolt model. The greatest amount of work on this one has been done by Norman Gottwald.[3] According to this model, the reason why archaeology shows little difference between Canaanites and Israelites is that most Israelites were originally native Canaanites. The major exceptions were the tribes of Benjamin, Ephraim, and Manasseh, who were the only part of Israel that experienced the Exodus. They entered Canaan at a time when many in the Canaanite lower class felt heavily the oppression of their rulers. Those lower class people joined forces with the incoming tribes and revolted against their political leaders. Breaking away from their city-states, they formed the Israelite confederacy in unoccupied parts of the country. The confederacy was based on the principle of social and economic equality. It was a conscious reaction to the former social position of most Israelites, who had been oppressed under the city-state system. The God of the new organization was Yahweh, who had been revealed as the God of the oppressed in the Exodus.

Today many scholars accept this revolt model, but there is increasing dissatisfaction with it in many circles.[4] The difficulty is that there is no real proof that the hypothesized revolt ever took place. However, the substantial contribution of the model is the recognition that the majority of Israelites could well have been Canaanites originally. So other scholars have accepted this feature, rejected the revolt concept, and developed other models of Israel's origin.

William Stiebing has proposed a rather promising paradigm.[5] He, first, demonstrates rather conclusively that there was a major drought throughout the Mediterranean region at the time of Israel's origin. Next, he shows that drought could account for those beginnings. At such a time, some cities fight with each other over the scarce food. This could explain the destruction of several Canaanite cities in this period. Some Canaanites may have left their home areas because food was too scarce there and moved into unoccupied parts of the land. There they encountered the small group of people who had taken part in the Exodus and recently entered the country. All of them formed Israel and accepted Yahweh as their God.

Why did early Israel not have social classes? The answer to that question will depend on whether one accepts the revolt model or one of the more recent ones. If the revolt model is correct, Israel did not have classes because they were reacting against their former oppression in the city-states. They were determined that no ruling class would exploit them again. If one of the more recent theories is right, there is no clear reason why Israel formed a classless society, just as there was no such reason in the models used before that of the revolt. But if there is no definite proof for a revolt, providing a reason for Israel's social structure is hardly sufficient cause for accepting that model. This is a question of history that must simply stand unanswered at present.

So, regardless of the reason for it, early Israel did not have social classes. This does not mean that there was total economic equality, but there were no sharp economic differences. Members of the people of Israel were free and had full civil rights. They had land holdings that they used for agriculture. This property was inherited from their ancestors and could not be sold to outsiders. What economic differences there were resulted from the vicissitudes of life. Things like crop failure and loss of family members in war harmed some families more than others.[6]

The great social change in Israel came with the monarchy, especially with King Solomon. He brought all of the expensive trappings of Near Eastern monarchy into the land. This included the royal household with a large harem, many children, attendants, and guards. It also added bureaucrats, a standing army, and extensive building projects. 1 Kings says: "Solomon's provision for one day was thirty cors [ca. four to six and one-half bushels] of choice flour, and sixty cors of meal, ten fat oxen, and twenty pasture-fed cattle, one hundred sheep, besides deer, gazelles, roebucks, and fatted fowl" (4:22-23). Besides the officials in Jerusalem, others were posted in the provinces as his representatives. They added to the mountain of expense.

How was this expansion paid for? The cost was met by heavy taxation and a policy of forced labor. According to 1 Kings: "King Solomon conscripted forced labor out of all Israel; the levy numbered thirty thousand men. He sent them to the Lebanon, ten thousand a month in shifts; they would be a month in the Lebanon and two months at home; . . . Solomon also had seventy thousand laborers and eighty thousand stonecutters in the hill country" (5:27-29 [NRSV 13-15]). Thus, Israelite men were forced to work without pay for the crown. Because of this policy, there were fewer workers at home on the farms and, consequently, less food was produced. Thus, farmers had less income at the very time that they were forced to pay new, exorbitant taxes to the government. Many were reduced to poverty.

Israel changed from a largely agricultural country to one that was both agricultural and commercial. Cities expanded with new groups of merchants, craftspeople, and former farmers.[7] Many of the farmers had lost their land to the new elite. This, then, is the time when classes developed in Israel with a sharp difference between them. There was a wealthy, upper class consisting of the monarchy with its administrative, religious, and military functionaries, as well as landholders, merchants, and small manufacturers, who benefited from state power. On the other hand, there was a poor, lower class made up of peasants, pastoralists, artisans, priests, slaves, and unskilled workers.[8] The upper class lived off the labor of the lower class. Thus, Solomon had introduced the same social structure into Israel that had evoked the Near Eastern statements about justice that we examined earlier. As the centuries passed, the disparity between the classes increased. Not only did the poor have to continue to pay for the structure which Solomon had created, but they had to support almost constant warfare between the kingdoms of Israel and Judah and with their neighbors. By the eighth century B.C.E., the time of the prophets Amos, Micah, and Isaiah, the gap between the classes was enormous. Archaeology has verified the differences. Excavations at Tirzah, an early capital of the northern kingdom, show uniform houses in the tenth century, the period of Solomon. By the eighth century, some houses were mansions, and others were hovels.[9] Expensive homes were in the western part of the city divided from the rest by a wall.[10] There prevailing western breezes cooled them while their odors blew toward the poor quarter. Similar disparity has also been revealed at Shechem.[11] In Samaria, the eighth-century capital of the north, the luxurious homes of the rich, decorated with imported ivory, have been uncovered.[12] Thus, archaeology shows Israel's class divisions. This, then, is the way in which the class structure of Israel developed and the setting of its appeals for social justice.

## The Deprived

Another matter of importance for our subsequent study of Scripture is the identification of the objects of social concern there. Who were the deprived in Israel? One group was the poor. There are several different words for them in Hebrew. The more prominent are *'ānî, 'ānāwîm, dal, 'ebyôn,* and *rāš.* All of these words refer to those in want, lacking enough for material needs. But they all also apply to people without the means to protect themselves from oppression.[13] They have become poor through injustice.

For example, *'ānî,* the word used most of those above in the Hebrew Bible, basically means "afflicted, bowed down." It refers to someone whose power has been lessened through an external force. Most often this means a person who has been wrongfully impoverished.[14] Some claimed formerly that the word *'ănāwîm* when used in the psalms did not mean physically poor. Those scholars claimed that the word was spiritualized and referred to the godly party in Israel, as opposed to the wicked. That argument has been largely abandoned today. It is recognized that the word is merely a linguistic variant of *'ānî*. It has the same connotations of material want and oppression.[15] At times psalms may include a spiritual component in their notion of poverty, but the material sense is not completely forgotten.

Similar to *'ānî*, *dal* primarily has the sense of "being low." It applies to those whose prosperity has been reduced and who lack physical and psychological strength. The *dal* is poor due to being unjustly deprived.[16] *'ebyôn* is often used for the very poor who are reduced to begging.[17] This term frequently occurs in lines paralleling those mentioning the *'ānî* or *dal* so that *'ebyôn* borrows their sense of unjust impoverishment. *Rāš* is a rather infrequent word, used mostly in the Wisdom literature. It may mean "dispossessed,"[18] and, thus, may have the connotation of losing one's belongings through injustice. In some contexts, the word is used without reference to oppression, but, in others, it is (Prov 29:13; Eccl 5:7).

Another group of people who are repeatedly singled out in the Hebrew Bible as objects for social justice are widows and fatherless children. In that society they needed the protection and economic support of an adult male. Males usually earned family incomes. A widow might receive the needed support from her husband's family through the practice of levirate marriage. According to that law men were obligated to marry their deceased brothers' widows if the dead had not fathered a son. The widow could also return to her own family. But if neither recourse were open to her, she and her children faced the prospect of exploitation and want.[19]

The final category of deprived people mentioned in the Hebrew Bible are the sojourners. The Scriptures use the term for foreign people living among the Israelites. They had privileges and responsibilities in the communities where they lived, but they did not have full rights and lacked protection. Their status was between that of natives and foreign people outside of Israel. In late writings they were naturalized aliens, proselytes. In most periods their position was somewhat insecure, and they consequently often suffered from poverty.[20]

## Legal Process

Much social injustice occurred in the lawcourt, so it will be helpful, next, to describe Israel's judicial procedure. In Israelite towns the area around the entrance gate was the center for all major political and commercial business. This was the marketplace and the primary site for visiting and exchanging news. The gate itself was a large, complicated structure containing a passageway and small rooms to the sides of it. These rooms were partially lined with benches for seating. The activities described above took place in these rooms and in the open space at the inside of the gate. This was also the site for legal proceedings.

Any individual involved in a case, such as either party to a dispute, an injured person, or the witness to an injury, could initiate a trial. That person called upon passing elders, leading citizens, to serve as judges. Even people involved in the case, such as the accuser or witnesses, could be judges. The parties to the case stood before the elders, who were seated, while anyone present at the gate could watch the proceedings. Both the accuser and the accused made their statements and could call witnesses to substantiate their contentions. Finally, the elders stood to give the verdict.

When the judges could reach no decision, there were three other ways of settling a case. Accused parties could undergo a physical ordeal to prove their innocence (e.g., Num 5:12-28). Also, a case could be settled by the drawing of lots, with the belief that God was giving the verdict. Or, finally, accused parties could take an oath of clearance. In this oath they pronounced curses on themselves if they were guilty of the crime. The assumption was that guilty people would not do this because they would fear receiving the curses. So a person who took the oath was regarded as innocent.

Common penalties for guilt were fines paid to the wronged party and flogging. Mutilation was rarely inflicted (Deut 25:11-12), and the death penalty was used in a limited number of situations. It was carried out by the whole community stoning the guilty party. Imprisonment was not a usual punishment until after the Exile.[21]

Under the Judean monarchy, this local system of justice was expanded. The ruler appointed professional judges, supposedly in every town (Deut 16:18-20; 2 Chr 19:4-11). There was also a high court in Jerusalem. Those presiding there were either priests and a judge (Deut 17:8-13) or priests, Levites, and heads of families (2 Chr 19:4-11). This was a court of first instance for inhabitants of Jerusalem and a court of appeal for other towns. If cases were considered too difficult for local courts, they could be referred to the Jerusalem one.[22]

## *The Monarch's Responsibility for Justice*

The royal involvement in the court system that we have just been considering implies the ruler's responsibility in this area. Judging was considered a key royal function in Israel. Over the Jerusalem court discussed above was the monarch's court although the lower court may have done much of the regular legal business. According to royal ideology, the ruler was the just person *par excellence*. Monarchs were the visible manifestation of the vindicating power of God.[23] God's wisdom was in them so that they could judge rightly (1 Kgs 3:28; Prov 16:10). Israel derived these ideas from its Near Eastern neighbors, and some of them had no written law codes because the ruler's role as a wise judge made them unnecessary. Thus, Egypt had no codified body of law until the Persian period.[24] Of course, Israel had law codes, but it seems that the monarch's judicial ability superseded them.[25] Rulers could judge on the basis of the divine wisdom in them, so they did not need to refer to written codes.

It was noted in the last chapter that rulers were a focus for justice to the unprotected in each of the Near Eastern countries. Israel's ideal also was that its monarch, having God's wisdom, was a righteous judge, especially of the needy. The following concepts were common throughout the Near East, and they also were present in Israel: In each country the god protected the weak. The ruler represented the deity in this function. The weak were easily robbed in courts because judges were partial or bribed by wealthy adversaries. So the highest protected the lowest.

Gods and rulers defended the rights of the needy. This was then expanded into a responsibility for ordinary people.[26] These ideas will reappear as we study biblical texts on social justice.

## Justice and Righteousness

Our discussion to this point has shown that God, rulers, and ordinary people were expected to be just. But what is justice in the biblical sense? The Hebrew Bible principally uses two terms when dealing with it: *mišpāṭ* and *ṣĕdāqāh*. English versions usually translate *mišpāṭ* with "justice" or "judgment." It is based on the verb *šāpaṭ* that is ordinarily translated "judge" but can also mean "govern" and "intervene to bring a situation to an appropriate resolution." *Mišpāṭ*, then, is the decision or action that results when someone *šāpaṭ*.[27] Thus, it can mean judgment when a person judges or justice when someone brings a situation to an appropriate resolution.

The implication of *mišpāṭ* is that rights are due to every individual in the community so that when a person *šāpaṭ*, those rights are to be upheld.[28] Thus, *mišpāṭ* is the restoration of a situation or environment which promoted equity and harmony in the community.[29] Consequently, the meaning of justice is somewhat different in Israel than in our culture. Here justice is behavior that conforms to an ethical or legal norm, so a judge decides cases on the basis of laws. In Israel, justice is based on relationships.[30] The meaning of this will be more clear as we examine *ṣĕdāqāh*.

English versions usually translate *ṣĕdāqāh* with "righteousness." The etymology of *ṣĕdāqāh* helps little in illuminating its meaning. The cognate Arabic root signifies straightness, hardness, or firmness. But none of these ideas can explain the variety of uses of the *ṣdq* root in the Hebrew Bible.[31]

A study of the uses of *ṣdq* reveals that it refers to a relationship between two parties and implies behavior which fulfills the claims arising from such an involvement. *Ṣdq* is, thus, the fulfillment of the demands of a relationship, with God or a person. There is no norm of righteousness outside of that personal involvement. When people fulfill the conditions imposed on them by relationships, they are righteous.[32] Every relationship has specific obligations. In Israel, there were connections between elders and their community, parents and children, and the wealthy and the poor. Each party owed something to the other, but righteousness made a greater claim on the stronger person. At times the weaker owed the stronger qualities like respect or obedience, but the stronger owed protection and material support.

Righteousness was a prescribed quality for an Israelite judge. That does not mean that he was to apply some formal standard of justice impartially. It means that he was rightly to satisfy the claims of the participants in a trial, brought forward from the relationships of their lives. In those relationships all had their own rights. It was the task of the righteous judge to make each one's right effective so that the good of everyone in the community was safeguarded.[33] The parties involved in a trial might also be called righteous. The righteous party was the one who had fulfilled the demands of the relationship in question or who had had rights taken away. It was the function of the judge to restore rights to those from whom they had been removed.[34]

With the background on Israel's social setting, we are prepared to analyze the portions of the Hebrew Bible that speak of social justice.

## Notes

1. John Bright, *A History of Israel,* 3rd ed. (Philadelphia: Westminster, 1981).

2. Martin Noth. *The History of Israel.* 2nd ed. (New York: Harper & Row, 1960).

3. Norman Gottwald, *The Tribes of Yahweh* (Maryknoll: Orbis, 1979).

4. J. M. Miller and John Hayes, *A History of Ancient Israel and Judah* (Philadelphia: Westminster, 1986) 74–79; N. P. Lemche, *Early Israel,* VTS 37 (Leiden: E. J. Brill, 1985) 32–33, 166, 195, 200, 207; Thomas Thompson, *Early History of the Israelite People,* Studies in the History of the Ancient Near East 4 (New York: E. J. Brill, 1992) 61–63.

5. William Stiebing, *Out of the Desert?* (Buffalo: Prometheus, 1989).

6. Willy Schottroff, "The Prophet Amos: A Socio-Historical Assessment of His Ministry," *God of the Lowly*, ed. Willy Schottroff and Wolfgang Stegemann, trans. Matthew O'Connell (Maryknoll: Orbis, 1984) 38.

7. L. John Topel, *The Way to Peace* (Maryknoll: Orbis, 1979) 17-18.

8. Norman Gottwald, "Social Class as an Analytic and Hermeneutical Category in Biblical Studies," *JBL* 112 (1993) 6.

9. James Mays, *Amos, A Commentary*, OTL (Philadelphia: Westminster, 1969) 2.

10. Schottroff, "Prophet Amos," 34.

11. Richard Sklba, *Pre-exilic Prophecy*, Message of Biblical Spirituality 3 (Collegeville: The Liturgical Press, 1990) 75.

12. Kathleen Kenyon, *Archaeology in the Holy Land* (New York: Frederick A. Praeger, 1960) 266-67.

13. J. Emmette Weir, "The Poor are Powerless: A Response to R. J. Coggins," *Exp Tim* 100 (1988) 13.

14. C. U. Wolf, "Poor," *IDB* 3:843; A. Kuschke, "Arm und reich im AT," *ZAW* 57 (1939) 49.

15. Wolf, "Poor," 843; J. David Pleins, "Poor, Poverty," *ABD* 5:413.

16. Wolf, "Poor," 843; H.-J. Fabry, *"Dal," TDOT* 3:220.

17. Ernst Bammel, *"Ptōchos," TDNT* 6:888–89.

18. Wolf, "Poor," 843.

19. F. Charles Fensham, "Widow, Orphan, and the Poor in Ancient Near Eastern Legal and Wisdom Literature," *JNES* 21 (1962) 136–37; Harry Hoffner, *"'almānāh," TDOT* 1: 288, 291.

20. T. Mauch, "Sojourner," *IDB* 4:397–98; John Spencer, "Sojourner," *ABD* 6:103.

21. Hans Boecker, *Law and the Administration of Justice in the Old Testament and Ancient East*, trans. Jeremy Moiser (Minneapolis: Augsburg, 1980) 31–38; Roland de Vaux, *Ancient Israel*, trans. John McHugh (New York: McGraw-Hill, 1961) 152–53, 156–60.

22. De Vaux, *Ancient Israel*, 153–54.

23. J. de Fraine, *L'aspect religieux de la royauté israélite*, Analecta Biblica 3 (Rome: Pontificio Istituto Biblico, 1954) 382.

24. John Wilson, *The Culture of Ancient Egypt* (Chicago: University of Chicago, 1951) 49–50.

25. Johannes Pedersen, *Israel: Its Life and Culture*, trans. Aslaug Moller (London: Oxford University, 1959) 3:80–81.

26. Fensham, "Widow, Orphan," 137–39.

27. Sklba, *Pre-exilic Prophecy*, 77.

28. Bruce Birch, *Let Justice Roll Down* (Louisville: Westminster, 1991) 155.

29. Temba Mafico, "Just, Justice," *ABD* 3:1128.

30. Bernhard Anderson, *The Eighth Century Prophets,* Proclamation Commentaries (Philadelphia: Fortress, 1978) 43.

31. E. R. Achtemeier, "Righteousness in the OT," *IDB* 4:80.

32. Ibid.

33. Walther Eichrodt, *Theology of the Old Testament*, trans. J. A. Baker (London: SCM Press, 1961) 1:241.

34. Achtemeier, "Righteousness in the OT," 81, 83.

# 3

# *Law Codes*[1]

Concern for social justice in Israel appears first in its law codes. This chapter examines the texts that show that concern.

## Social Setting

The examination will be clarified if a few preliminary matters are considered first. One is the social setting of the statements about justice in the codes. Past research on this question has led to one basic item of agreement and opposite, subsequent conclusions. As we saw in chapter 1, most interpreters are agreed that Israel received its concern for social justice from the Near Eastern cultures surrounding it. However, it is difficult to know how to relate this fact to the references to social justice in Israelite law codes. What Near Eastern literature and Israelite codes have in common is their content. The forms through which it is conveyed differ. Near Eastern literature normally expresses its concern for the deprived in forms like confessions, instructions, and hymn-petitions, rather than through legal statements.[2] Another problem is raised by the social setting of the Near Eastern references. They are regularly based on a royally dominated social structure. Do the Israelite laws derive from the same setting?

A few scholars believe that they do. These authors contend that the parts of Israelite legal codes dealing with justice for the oppressed were added during the monarchic period.[3] Injustice was not a particular problem for Israel until that time. As chapter 2 showed, there is general agreement that this was the period when sharp differences in social class arose. Harriet Havice explains that then laws were created on the basis of Near Eastern wisdom instructions about the underprivileged.[4] Thus, she explains the similar content but different forms of Near Eastern and Israelite statements on justice.

However, many scholars disagree with this view. They believe that at least some of these laws derive from the early, tribal period of Israel's history.[5] H. E. von Waldow explains the similar content of Near Eastern and Israelite statements by showing that the substance of some Near Eastern and Israelite writings both originated among ancient, Semitic clans.[6] Also, he demonstrates that there was always a need for some laws on social justice because there were always some in Israel who were not economically secure, namely the sojourner, widow, and fatherless child. He partially agrees with the first group of scholars by saying that some laws on the deprived were added to the codes when extremes of poverty and wealth developed under the monarchy.[7] So it is likely that the laws being analyzed in this chapter developed during a long period of Israel's history extending from its beginnings to the monarchic period. The laws arose from quite different social settings, including an early period of relative equality and a late period of great economic disparity.

## The Nature of the Law Codes

Another preliminary matter of importance is our assumptions about the nature of the law codes, which will clarify the following analysis of their injunctions regarding deprived people. Although a few of these laws occur in other legal parts of the Pentateuch, most of them are in the three basic codes. The oldest is the Book of the Covenant (Exod 20:22–23:33) which originated at the time of the tribal confederacy and reflects the agricultural life of that period. The second is the Deuteronomic Code (Deut 12–26). An oral form of this material was probably originally used as part of the covenant renewal ceremony at Shechem. After the destruction of the northern kingdom in 722 B.C.E., these laws were taken to Jerusalem where they were adapted to circumstances there and put into written form. This code seems dependent on the earlier Book of the Covenant. The final collection is the Holiness Code (Lev 17–26). These laws were gathered by priests in the Jerusalem Temple and reduced to writing shortly before or after the destruction of that city in 587 B.C.E. There is a development of concern for justice to the oppressed in the evolution of these codes. The Book of the Covenant has some striking statements on this subject, but their number is small. These are Israel's earliest texts on social justice, where Israel is borrowing and adapting Near Eastern statements for the first time. There is a great increase in the number of such laws in the Deuteronomic Code. By this time the prophets and others have contributed to Israel's legacy on social justice, and Deuteronomy has a large base on which to build. The Holiness Code has a significant amount of injunctions on justice, but their total is smaller than that of the previous collection. Also, Leviticus 25 has the only noticeably new thoughts on the topic. Thus, the first and last collections will provide some important data for this investigation, but the Deuteronomic Code will furnish the most.

Lastly, the form of the commands dealing with the deprived in all of these codes is usually apodictic law, simple statements commanding or forbidding certain behavior. These laws are often interspersed with motivating comments, but it is generally agreed that these motivations are secondary additions.[8]

### Social Justice

The commands prohibit oppressive actions and call for positive deeds toward the deprived. A few of the prohibitions oppose mistreatment generally. Exodus 22:21 and 23:9 forbid oppressing the sojourner and 22:22, the widow and fatherless. Deuteronomy 10:19 makes the command about the sojourner more far-reaching by converting it into a positive injunction. The reader is to love the sojourners, not merely refrain from mistreating them. Leviticus 19:33-34 contains both thoughts and adds that Israel should look upon the sojourner as one of themselves and love him or her as much as oneself. Leviticus 24:22 further specifies that sojourners and natives are to be governed by one law. Thus, these commands reveal high ethical sensitivity in not only providing total justice for people easily misused but also in calling for equality with and love toward them.

Next, the laws become specific in forbidding actions that would deprive the poor. Exodus 22:26 discusses pledges, material objects given as collateral for loans. It insists that garments given in pledge are to be returned before sundown. Without a cloak a poor person would have no covering for the night. The Deuteronomic Code extends this law. It simply prohibits the use of a widow's garment as a pledge (Deut 24:17). The code also forbids a creditor to go into a debtor's house to fetch a pledge (24:10-11). The debtor's dignity is preserved since the debtor is allowed to choose an appropriate object and bring it out.

The laws on interest similarly protect the deprived. In the Book of the Covenant Israel is not permitted to collect interest from the poor who borrow (Exod 22:25). The term used probably signifies interest paid in advance.[9] Deuteronomy's addition to this law does not affect the needy particularly since it merely prohibits interest toward any Israelite but permits it toward foreigners (23:19-20). But the Holiness Code increases the protection of the deprived by forbidding that they repay interest with a loan *(tarbit)* as well as paying it in advance (Lev 25:35-37). The safety which such laws provided the poor becomes clearer when it is observed that the interest charged in the Near East sometimes was as high as one-third or one-half of the original loan.[10]

The laws on measure likewise prevented the needy from being deprived. As we saw in chapter 1, this was an earlier concern of Near Eastern texts. The Instruction of Amenemope forbade false weights since dishonest merchants used them to deprive the needy of merchandise for which they paid. The Deuteronomic Code went further and called for just measures of both weight and quantity (25:13-15). The Holiness Code added length and liquid quantity to be sure that all possibilities would be covered (Lev 19:35-36). Similar protection was offered by Deuteronomy's injunction against moving a landmark at the border of a neighbor's property (19:14, 27:17), another earlier Near Eastern concern. A simple marker indicated where one person's property ended, and another's began. An unscrupulous person could move landmarks into the property of poor neighbors and thereby steal some of their land, so this was forbidden. Also, Deuteronomy commanded that poor, hired servants be paid their wages on the day they were earned (24:14-15). And

the Holiness Code regulated the treatment of needy Israelites
who sold themselves into another's service (Lev 25:39-43). The
latter was not to bully them. Those who sold themselves were to
be treated as hired servants and not as slaves, for they were
Yahweh's slaves and no one else's.

The largest number of laws censoring action that impoverished the poor had to do with injustice in the law court. Exodus
23:6 forbade perverting justice against the poor and was apparently addressed to judges.[11] Deuteronomy 24:17 gave the same
command about the sojourner and fatherless, and 27:19 pronounced a curse on those transgressing this command toward
those two types of individuals or the widow. Other laws became more specific in delineating the types of behavior that
produced injustice. According to the present text of Exodus
23:3, judges were not to be partial to the poor in their suits.
It is surprising that the earliest, written law on partiality would
oppose favoring the poor since it was more common that
judges were partial to the rich. Consequently, some have sug-
gested that the present text is incorrect and that the passage
originally opposed favoring the great *(gādōl)*, rather than the
poor *(dal)*.[12] But in any case, subsequent injunctions outlawed
partiality toward either group (Deut 1:17, Lev 19:15). Also,
some prohibitions spoke against bribes (Exod 23:8, Deut
16:19) since they were an evident cause of favoritism. Recall
that all of these matters, just judgment of the weak, lack of partiality, and bribes, were the subject of earlier Near Eastern
statements.

Another type of unjust, court behavior decried was false witnessing (Exod 23:1-2). The Deuteronomic Code expanded the
original law on this subject at length (Deut 19:15-21). For one
thing, Deuteronomy protected the accused by mandating that
more than one witness give evidence. Also, it pronounced that
the penalty for false witnessing would be the same as that which
threatened the defendant. And it stated that Israel was not to pity
one giving false testimony. This command enhances the heinous-
ness of the crime over the original injunction in Exodus against
being a false witness. Deuteronomy does not imagine that readers would be guilty of such an act, only that they would have to
react to it in another.[13]

All of the prohibitions above, then, forbid behavior which would impoverish the deprived. There are also laws which call for positive acts toward them. Several of these commands have to do with giving to the poor in various ways, a favorite Near Eastern subject. Deuteronomy 15:7-11 is an extended passage on this topic. The reader is instructed to lend to a needy person whatever is required (v. 8). Then the passage continues with repeated injunctions to give to such a person freely. The text is basically concerned with loans, but in some cases they are virtual gifts because they will be cancelled at the year of release that occurs every seven years. Likewise, Leviticus 25:35-37 commands the Israelites to strengthen those who become poor and reminds those who lend to the needy that there is to be no interest charged.

The laws insisting that farmers leave gleanings in the field were another method of giving to the poor (Deut 24:19-22; Lev 19:9-10; 23:22). The original reason for this custom was probably to leave an offering for the fertility spirits of the soil.[14] But all of the Israelite codes convert that custom into a means of providing sustenance for the deprived.

The rule of the Sabbath Year, that farmers leave their fields fallow every seventh year, was similar. The initial reason for this regulation was probably to return the land to its original state and to assert Yahweh's direct ownership of it.[15] But the earliest code, the Book of the Covenant, makes this practice a way to feed the needy (Exod 23:10-11). In the Deuteronomic Code the procedure for observing the year has changed, but it has remained a method of helping the poor. Now there is no law mandating leaving the land fallow, but creditors are to dissolve all debts in the seventh year (Deut 15:1-3). By this time poor farmers would have suffered under the old rule. The monarchy placed such a heavy tax burden on them that they could not afford to lose a year of agriculture. The new law removed this problem and helped them by cancelling their debts.[16] This was a practical application of the earlier command found in the Instruction of Amenemope to reduce the size of the poor's debts. The adaptation of the Sabbath Year regulation in the Holiness Code only minimally benefited the deprived (Lev 25:2-7). This code again made fallow land the object of this rule. The farmer's household was allowed to eat what grew of itself. But at least one group of needy were included among the beneficiaries, the sojourners.

The Deuteronomic Code developed still another means of providing charity for the poor. There was an annual tithe of agricultural produce used for cultic purposes (14:22-27). Every three years, this tithe was kept in the communities where it was grown and distributed to the needy (14:28-29).[17]

In addition to the laws above that call for gifts to the deprived, there are other positive commands that produce greater equality between rich and poor. The Sabbath commandment in the Decalogue and the Book of the Covenant is one of these (Exod 20:10; 23:12; Deut 5:14). In the list of those who are to observe this day, the 'sojourner is explicitly mentioned. And Deuteronomy makes clear that the intention of this stipulation is that such designated people may have as much chance to rest as propertied Israelites. Likewise, the Deuteronomic Code specifically includes the sojourner, the fatherless, and the widow among those who may celebrate the feasts of Weeks and Booths (16:11, 14). They are equal to monied people in their right to enjoy the festivals.

Other commands provide for greater economic parity between rich and poor. Thus, a number of cultic laws permit needy people to bring less expensive sacrifices (Lev 12:8; 14:21-22). For example, there are three levels of penalties for sins depending on one's wealth: a sheep, two doves, and flour (5:7, 11). Also, the Holiness Code aimed at establishing widespread economic equality through the institution of the Jubilee Year although scholars are disagreed about whether it was ever observed.[18] In any case, the intention of the regulation was that land sold would return to its original owners and that Israelite bondservants would be released (Lev 25:10). Such a practice would have provided equity since the poor would have gained property and freedom from service without price, at the expense of the rich.

### Motivation

Thus, the Israelite law codes show a great deal of concern with the plight of the deprived. The laws attempt to rectify this problem by preventing mistreatment of the poor and by mandating improvement of their lot through giving and equalizing wealth and privileges. The codes also provide secondary motivation to stimulate people to obey these regulations. One group of incentives appeals to retribution. Some of them threaten disaster for disobedience (Deut 15:9; 24:15). Exodus 22:23-24 is one of the most explicit and warns that Yahweh will hear the cry of the afflicted widow or orphan and kill their oppressor. Numerous retribution passages promise blessing for obedience. Most of them occur in Deuteronomy and predict the typical Deuteronomic blessings of possession of Canaan with success and long life there (e.g., 15:10; 16:20; 25:15). Referring to retribution as a motivation has both negative and positive implications. The negative aspect is that such an incentive sometimes attempts to force people into obedience through the fear of disaster or the hope of blessing. Thus, it does not value highly people's willingness to respond to God. On the other hand, at times there is an element of realism in appealing to retribution. Certain moral acts do lead to negative or positive results.

Another group of motivations refers to God's authority. Deuteronomy 25:16 simply states that those who use dishonest weights are an abomination to Yahweh, with the implication that readers would not choose God's abhorrence. The rest of the uses of this kind of incentive are in the Holiness Code. Israel is to observe the Jubilee Year and not sell property permanently because the land belongs to God (Lev 25:23). Israelites are not to be sold as slaves because they are Yahweh's slaves (25:42). And the most frequent way in which this code appeals to God's authority is merely to conclude a law with the words, "I am Yahweh your God" (e.g., 19:10; 23:22). Basing a command on Yahweh's authority calls upon the relationship that exists between God and the Israelites. If they have learned through experience to trust Yahweh, they will realize that a command God gives is for the best, and they will respond to it positively. This kind of motivation takes seriously their freedom to obey or disobey and expresses the confidence that they will respond positively because of their closeness to God.[19]

Other types of motivations also show a high regard for the ethical sensitivity of their readers. Some of these incentives call upon Israelites' compassion or reasonableness. So Exodus 22:27

urges them to return garments taken in pledge before sundown because such clothing is the poor's only covering for the night. Employers are to pay workers on the day they earn their wages because laborers are poor and rely on earnings for their livelihood (Deut 24:15). Exodus 23:8 shows that it is not reasonable to take a bribe because it blinds clear-sighted judges and perverts the words of those in the right. And readers are to give freely to the deprived because there will always be a need for such charity. The poor will never cease to exist in Israel (Deut 15:11).

Another kind of motivation that also recognizes people's willingness to make responsible choices appeals to Israel's experience in the Exodus, one of the two bases of Israel's social concern examined in chapter 1. Many of these clauses exhort readers to pity the deprived because in Egypt the Israelites learned how the needy feel. These statements remind readers that they were sojourners (e.g., Exod 23:9; Lev 19:34) or slaves (e.g., Deut 16:12; 24:22) in Egypt. Other clauses urge obedience because God brought Israel out of Egypt in the Exodus (e.g., Deut 5:15; 24:18; Lev 25:38). The point of these assertions is that readers are to care for the weak out of gratitude for God's deliverance.

A final type of positive motive calls upon people to give such care because of the way that God reacts to the deprived. People are to imitate God's feelings and actions toward the needy. Exodus 22:27 exhorts readers to be compassionate to the poor because Yahweh is compassionate. And Deuteronomy 10:17-18 develops this concept in detail. Yahweh is not partial and takes no bribe. God acts justly for the fatherless and widow. God loves and gives food and clothing to the sojourner. Verse 19 makes the point of this description explicit. Readers are to love the sojourner. The whole passage is an appeal to imitate God's love, charity, and just acts toward the poor. Israel has here taken the Near Eastern idea that social concern begins with the gods and enriched it with Israel's own theology.

It is apparent, then, that the Israelite law codes are a fertile source of thought about social justice. They picture methods by which the Israelites tried to aid the deprived. Underlying specific approaches were broader attempts to prevent unjust acts, to stimulate giving, and at least partially to equalize the position of the rich and poor. And particularly the motivations used in the codes that recognized people's willingness to make responsible decisions have value for us. Those were the appeals to recognize God's authority, to have compassion, to act out of gratitude to God's saving actions, and to imitate God's concern for the weak. Thus, the ancient legal codes of the Pentateuch are a valuable part of the Hebrew Bible's teaching on justice to the poor.

## Notes

1. An earlier version of this chapter appeared as "Social Justice in the Israelite Law Codes," *Word & World* 4 (1984) 299–306. Material from it is used here with permission of the publisher.

2. Harriet Havice, "The Concern for the Widow and the Fatherless in the Ancient Near East" (Ph.D. diss., Yale University, 1979) 12, 173.

3. F. Charles Fensham, "Widow, Orphan, and the Poor in Ancient Near Eastern Legal and Wisdom Literature," *JNES* 21 (1962) 137–39; Havice, "Concern for the Widow," 206.

4. Havice, "Concern for the Widow," 204.

5. Martin Noth, *The Laws in the Pentateuch and Other Studies,* trans. D. Ap-Thomas (Philadelphia: Fortress, 1966) 33, 60; Erhard Gerstenberger, *Wesen und Herkunft des "apodiktischen Rechts,"* WMANT 20 (Neukirchen: Neukirchener Verlag, 1965); H. Eberhard von Waldow, "Social Responsibility and Social Structure in Early Israel," *CBQ* 32 (1970) 184–85.

6. Von Waldow, "Social Responsibility," 184–85.

7. Ibid., 194–99.

8. Havice, "Concern for the Widow," 202.

9. G. Barrois, "Debt, Debtor," *IDB* 1:809.

10. Ibid.

11. J. W. McKay, "Exodus xxiii 1–3, 6–8: A Decalogue for the Administration of Justice in the City Gate," *VT* 21 (1971) 324; Brevard Childs, *The Book of Exodus,* OTL (Philadelphia: Westminster, 1974) 482.

12. Martin Noth, *Exodus, A Commentary,* trans. J. S. Bowden, OTL (Philadelphia: Westminster, 1962) 189.

13. Calum Carmichael, *The Laws of Deuteronomy* (Ithaca: Cornell University, 1974) 116.

14. Martin Noth, *Leviticus, A Commentary,* trans. J. E. Anderson, OTL, rev. ed. (Philadelphia: Westminster, 1977) 141.

15. Ibid., 186.

16. Gerhard von Rad, *Deuteronomy, A Commentary,* trans. Dorothea Barton, OTL (Philadelphia: Westminster, 1966) 106.

17. H. Guthrie, "Tithe," *IDB* 4:654.

18. J. Morgenstern, "Jubilee, Year of," *IDB* 2:1002; A. van Selms, "Jubilee, Year of," *IDBSupp.* 497.

19. Claus Westermann, *Creation,* trans. John Scullion (Philadelphia: Fortress, 1974) 89–91.

# 4

# *The Prophetic Books*

## *Background of Key Prophets*

The most striking statements on social justice in the Hebrew Bible occur in the prophetic books, which we shall analyze next. Although there are significant sayings in other books, four prophets have the most to say about this topic: Amos, Micah, Isaiah, and Jeremiah. It will aid our analysis if we look first at the background of these four men.

Amos was chronologically the first prophet after whom a book was named, and he prophesied around 760 to 750 B.C.E. As we saw in chapter 2, the eighth century was the time by which the greatest disparity between rich and poor had developed in Israel. Jeroboam II was on the throne of the northern kingdom, and Azariah was king of the south. This was a glorious time for both countries. The northern kingdom, Israel, was successful militarily and had pushed its northern boundary back to where it had been in Solomon's period. There was peace with the southern kingdom of Judah, a rare occurrence. Judah had also expanded militarily at the expense of its southern neighbors. Both nations were enjoying prosperity; Israel was experiencing the greatest economic growth it had known since the time of Solomon. But prosperity was only for the rich, and the poor suffered under their oppression.

Amos came from the Judean town of Tekoa, a little south of Jerusalem, but he prophesied in Israel. Recent scholars agree that

31

Amos was a wealthy man.[1] He is called a "sheepbreeder" in Amos 1:1, a term designating the owner of an estate who hires shepherds. The only other time that the term is used in the Hebrew Bible, 2 Kings 3:4, it refers to the king of Moab. In 7:14 Amos identifies himself as a caretaker of sycamores, but there are none near his hometown. So he probably travelled to supervise sycamore labor elsewhere. Being wealthy, he was an educated person. His speech shows that he was gifted in oral skills. He knew Wisdom materials, the history of Israel's neighbors, and Israel's social situation and religious traditions. His demands on Israel were based on the Book of the Covenant,[2] which contained Israel's first calls for social justice.

The next significant prophet for our purposes, Micah, was also a Judean and prophesied there. Micah 1:1 places him in the reigns of Jotham, Ahaz, and Hezekiah, the Judean kings after Azariah. This period extends from 742 to 687 B.C.E. Although Micah probably did not prophesy during this entire period, his message fits well within it. Since 1:5 is directed against Samaria, Micah began his work before 722, when the capital of Israel fell. Jeremiah 26:18 corroborates that he prophesied in the time of Hezekiah.

During the reign of Ahaz (735-715), conditions worsened in Judah. Ahaz became an ally of Tiglath-pileser, the Assyrian emperor, at the price of an enormous tribute. Tiglath-pileser conquered Syria in 732, and his successors destroyed the northern kingdom of Israel in 722. Judah's next king, Hezekiah, was one of its best rulers. He carried on a gradual reform of the nation, combatting the idolatry that Ahaz had encouraged, including the worship of the Assyrian gods. In the eyes of the Assyrians, repudiation of their gods was political revolt—precisely what Hezekiah intended. The Assyrians could not let this revolt go unrequited, and in 701 Sennacherib attacked Judah. Hezekiah paid him off with a large tribute, and he withdrew.

Micah was from a town called Moresheth in the hill country of Judah, twenty-two miles southwest of Jerusalem. Moresheth was near the border between Judah and Philistia and thus was open to attack. Judah's first king, Rehoboam, had fortified the town, so it was more than a pastoral village. Military and administrative officials of the court were present there.[3] Micah may have been an elder of Moresheth. At least, he was likely one of the rural upper class.[4] His words reveal the same kind of linguistic giftedness and knowledge that Amos had. Micah may have begun prophesying in Moresheth, but it is likely that he then went to Jerusalem and did most of his speaking there. Jeremiah 26:19 suggests that his preaching influenced Hezekiah, who ruled in Jerusalem.

Isaiah prophesied under the same kings as Micah and was a Jerusalemite. He began his prophetic work in the year that Azariah died and continued until about 734 in the reign of Ahaz. Then he withdrew from his task until the death of Ahaz in 715. Subsequently he reemerged as a prophet under Hezekiah and continued as such until about 701. He had a wife who is called a prophetess in Isaiah 8:3. It is unknown whether that term means that she was the wife of a prophet or a prophet herself. The couple had two sons whom Isaiah gave symbolic names: Shearjashub, "a remnant will return," and Maher-shalal-hash-baz, "the spoil speeds, the booty hastens."

Although a few scholars doubt that anything can be known about Isaiah's personal status,[5] most accept the traditional view that he was an aristocrat.[6] He had access to the king and leading members of the royal court. He regularly uses language from the Wisdom tradition, suggesting that he may have been educated at that court. Also, he was a gifted poet and had knowledge of history and current events.

Finally, Jeremiah functioned as a prophet for an extremely long time. He began during the reign of Josiah, around the year 626, and continued until after the fall of Jerusalem in 587. Josiah's grandfather Manasseh had introduced a great deal of idolatry into Judah, and Jeremiah opposed it during his early period. Then Josiah carried out an extensive religious reform of the country, which Jeremiah apparently supported and during which he probably did not prophesy. During Josiah's reign, the Assyrian Empire began to crumble. He died trying to aid the process by attacking the pharaoh of Egypt, an ally of Assyria. Shortly afterward, the Babylonians defeated the Egyptians and became the new rulers of the Near East. Under them Jehoiakim became king of Judah and was a notorious tyrant. Jeremiah reappeared as a prophet during his rule, attacking the immorality in the country. Ultimately Jehoiakim revolted against Babylon and died before they retaliated. They besieged and defeated Jerusalem after his son Jehoiachin had reigned for only three months. Jehoiachin and the leaders of Judah were deported to Babylon, and Zedekiah became the new king. He ruled for eleven years until he also revolted against Babylon. This time the Babylonians destroyed Jerusalem and took a larger group of Judeans into exile. Jeremiah remained in Jerusalem until a group of Judeans assassinated the Babylonian–appointed governor. When they fled to Egypt, Jeremiah went with them and apparently died there.

Jeremiah had originally come from Anathoth, a village four miles north of Jerusalem. Like the previous three prophets, he was also an educated person of high position. He was descended from a priestly family (1:1) and at Jerusalem's court was part of a powerful political party. This was the group that favored coexistence with Babylon and contained upper-class families like those of Shaphan (26:24) and Neraiah (32:12; 51:59).[7] That Jeremiah had wealth is indicated by his ownership of land (ch. 32) and his ability to afford his own scribe.[8]

It is striking that all four of the prophets who said most about social justice were people of means. Although the poor undoubtedly cared most about the subject because it existentially involved them, apparently not all upper-class people in Israel were insensitive to their plight. These four prophets were moved enough to risk trouble with their own class by taking the side of the needy.

## Social Injustice

The largest number of statements by the prophets on justice are descriptions of problems. A few are rather general. For example, the prophet whose words were first written, Amos, says of his hearers:

> Ah, you that turn justice to wormwood,
> and bring righteousness to the ground (5:7)!

Wormwood was a plant with a sharply bitter pulp, and so, Amos' listeners were changing the sweetness of justice to the bitterness of injustice. On another occasion Amos addresses the wives of court officials, owners of large estates, and merchants living in the capital of Israel with the words[9]

> Hear this word, you cows of Bashan
> who are on Mount Samaria,
> who oppress the poor, who crush the needy,
> who say to their husbands,
> "Bring something to drink!" (4:1)

Bashan was the territory on the east side of the Sea of Galilee that had the reputation of being the best pasture land in Israel. Amos was calling the wealthy women of the capital fat cows, which undoubtedly did not endear him to his audience. But he was more concerned about the issue of justice than winning their favor.

That kind of concern drove Micah to even greater lengths. Perhaps in the outer court of the Jerusalem Temple, he proclaimed to the officials responsible for legal justice:[10]

> Should you not know justice?—
> you who hate the good and love the evil,
> who tear the skin off my people,
> and the flesh off their bones;
> who eat the flesh of my people,
> flay their skin off them,
> break their bones in pieces,
> and chop them up like meat in a kettle,
> like flesh in a caldron (3:1-3).

Although the fervor of the prophets often compelled them to speak extremely, none of them ever spoke as coarsely as this.[11] But Micah could not talk moderately about the damage that unjust judges were doing to the poor.

A final example of a general statement comes from the prophet Habakkuk. He laments:

> O Lord, how long shall I cry for help,
> and you will not listen?
> Or cry to you "Violence!"
> and you will not save?
> Why do you make me see wrong-doing

and look at trouble?
Destruction and violence are before me;
strife and contention arise.
So the law becomes slack
and justice never prevails.
The wicked surround the righteous—
therefore judgment comes forth perverted (1:2-4).

Habakkuk complained out of the agony he felt over the abuses of justice that characterized the reign of Jehoiakim.[12]

When the prophets become more specific, they bring up some of the same issues that the law codes raised. One of these was the matter of pledges, items turned over as collateral for loans. Amos condemns those who "lay themselves down beside every altar on garments taken in pledge" (2:8). Recall that the Book of the Covenant forbade keeping a garment overnight (Exod 22:26) and that Deuteronomy simply prohibited using a widow's garment as a pledge (24:17). So Amos' hearers have been violating these laws at the expense of the poor. In giving examples of righteous behavior, Ezekiel once lists restoring a pledge to a debtor (18:7) and once goes farther and commends exacting no pledge at all (v. 16). In the same passages Ezekiel says that it is righteous not to take interest paid in advance or repaid with a loan (vv. 8, 17). When lending to the poor, the former was forbidden in Exodus 22:25, and the latter, in Leviticus 25:35-37.

Another concern of the law codes and earlier Near Eastern texts that resurfaces in the prophets is just measure (e.g., Hos 12:8 [NRSV v. 7]; Mic 6:10-11). However, observe the increase in indignation on this subject in this oracle of Amos:

Hear this, you that trample on the needy,
and bring to ruin the poor of the land,
saying, "When will the new moon be over
so that we may sell grain;
and the sabbath,
so that we may offer wheat for sale?
We will make the ephah small and the shekel great,
and practice deceit with false balances" (8:4-5).

The new moon and sabbath were both festival occasions when no work was allowed.[13] Amos pictures wealthy merchants chafing at the bit on these days because they want to get back to the marketplace so that they can go on cheating the poor. They cheat by using false measures. They use an *ephah,* the bushel basket for holding grain, that is smaller than standard size so that they can sell buyers less than they pay for. The buyers' money is weighed on scales, but the weight that the sellers put on the other side, the *shekel,* is larger than expected. Thus, buyers must pay too much money and are cheated once again. Archaeologists have actually discovered eighth-century shops at Tirzah in northern Israel with different size weights used for buying or selling.[14] Amos also mentions "false balances," another method of cheating with scales. Sellers would distort them by bending down one side of the crossbeam so that buyers would have to put on still more money to balance them.[15]

We have seen that in the Near East generally and in Israel's law codes the specific justice concern that received the greatest amount of attention was injustice in the law court. This is also true of the prophets. Isaiah said:

> Woe to those who decree iniquitous decrees,
> and the writers who keep writing oppression,
> to turn aside the needy from justice
> and to rob the poor of my people of their right,
> that widows may be their spoil,
> and that they may make the fatherless their prey (10:1-2 RSV)!

This is directed to officials in Jerusalem who administer justice. Isaiah condemns them for writing judgments about poor individuals that deprive them of their rights.[16] A post-exilic addition to Isaiah attacks those[17] "who by a word make a man out to be an offender, and lay a snare for him who reproves in the gate, and with an empty plea turn aside him who is in the right" (29:21 RSV). We saw in chapter 2 that the gate of towns was the site where law cases were judged. This text opposes those who pervert justice in that setting.

Similarly, this is the prophet Zephaniah's description of Jerusalem's condition before Josiah's reform:

> The officials within it are roaring lions;
> its judges are evening wolves that leave nothing until
> the morning (3:3).

Zephaniah here is ironically reversing the usual positive use of these animals' names (e.g., Gen 49:9, 27) in order to portray graphically the destruction caused by unjust judges.[18] Finally, in the post-exilic period Zechariah recalls that these were the kind of words proclaimed by the earlier prophets,[19] "Render true judgments, show kindness and mercy to one another; do not oppress the widow, the orphan, the alien, or the poor" (7:9-10). He sees fair judgment of the needy as a central message of the previous prophets.

Bribery was a particular reason for injustice in the law court which was forbidden in Near Eastern statements and Israelite law codes. The prophets also frequently condemn its use (e.g., Amos 5:12; Mic 3:9-11; Isa 5:23). Isaiah says of Jerusalem:

> Your princes are rebels and companions of thieves.
> Everyone loves a bribe and runs after gifts.
> They do not defend the orphan,
> and the widow's cause does not come before them (1:23).

Next, we saw in chapter 2 that the ruler was expected to be an ideally just judge in Israel and in the Near East generally. Jeremiah takes up this subject both negatively and positively. First, he addresses these words to the tyrant king Jehoiakim and his officials:

> Hear the word of the LORD, O King of Judah sitting on the throne of David—you, and your servants, and your people who enter these gates. Thus says the LORD: Act with justice and righteousness, and deliver from the hand of the oppressor anyone who has been robbed. And do no wrong or violence to the alien, the orphan, and the widow, or shed innocent blood in this place (22:2-3).

Jehoiakim is to fulfill the ancient ideal of kingship, but Jeremiah gives this reminder because it is clear that the king has been doing just the opposite.

In 22:13-17 Jeremiah attacks Jehoiakim more directly for the same reasons:

> Woe to him who builds his house by unrighteousness,
> and his upper rooms by injustice;
> who makes his neighbors work for nothing,
> and does not give them their wages; . . .
> Are you a king because you compete in cedar?
> Did not your father eat and drink and do justice and
> righteousness?
> Then it was well with him.
> He judged the cause of the poor and needy;
> then it was well.
> Is not this to know me? says the LORD.
> But your eyes and heart are only on your dishonest gain,
> for shedding innocent blood,
> and for practicing oppression and violence.

At this moment the problem with Jehoiakim is that he is using forced labor to renovate his old palace or to build a new one.[20] Like Solomon before him, he is compelling Israelites to work for the crown without wages. While condemning him for this, Jeremiah contrasts him with his father Josiah. Josiah fulfilled the ideal of kingship, rightly judging the needy, but Jehoiakim only practices oppression.

Besides calling for justice, the law codes and Near Eastern texts appealed for gifts to the poor. It is striking how seldom the prophetic books do the same. The prophets may have felt that it is not time to ask the unjust to be charitable while they are cheating the poor. Let the oppressors give the needy what they deserve, not what the unjust can comfortably do without. When the subject of charity comes up in the prophets, it does so in particular ways. For example, Ezekiel mentions it in a list of righteous acts. The devout person "gives his bread to the hungry and covers the naked with a garment" (18:7, 16). A disciple of Ezekiel brings up charity when recalling the sin of Sodom.[21] He says to Jerusalem: "This was the guilt of your sister Sodom: she and her daughters had pride, excess of food, and prosperous ease, but did not aid the poor and needy" (Ezek 16:49). The final occurrence appears in a sage's addition to Isaiah.[22] He states that it is typical of the fool

> to leave the craving of the hungry unsatisfied,
> and to deprive the thirsty of drink (32:6).

So none of the references to giving to the poor in the prophetic books occur in relation to events that the prophets are experiencing. The references are all more general.

. The discussion to this point has described the various unjust and uncharitable acts that the prophets indict. Next, they go on to reveal the results of these acts for the rich and the poor. The injustice of the wealthy has made them richer still. Particularly Amos describes their luxury, referring several times to their magnificent houses (5:11; 6:11). In 3:15 he pictures Yahweh saying

> I will tear down the winter house as well as the summer house;
> and the houses of ivory shall perish,
> and the great houses shall come to an end.

The rich were wealthy enough to own two houses, one located in a warmer place for winter and the other in a cooler place for summer. In regard to the "houses of ivory," in Samaria archaeologists have found furniture decorated with reliefs carved into ivory plates.[23]

Amos mentions that furniture in another portrayal of the wealthy's luxury:

> Alas for those who lie on beds of ivory,
> and lounge on their couches,
> and eat lambs from the flock,
> and calves from the stall;
> who sing idle songs to the sound of harp,
> and like David improvise on instruments of music;
> who drink wine from bowls,
> and anoint themselves with the finest oils,
> but are not grieved over the ruin of Joseph (6:4-6)!

Until now Israelites had generally sat on rugs or seats to eat, but the rich have advanced to dining on ivory-inlaid couches.[24] Like today, they eat veal from a stall where calves are kept from moving freely so that their meat remains tender.[25] The wealthy enjoy these and the other luxuries described but do not think about the destruction from God that they are bringing on themselves.

And how has the growing wealth of the rich affected the poor? The wealthy have more luxury because they have stripped other citizens of their possessions (Isa 3:13-15; Mic 2:8-9). Micah says:

> Alas for those who devise wickedness
> and evil deeds on their beds!
> When the morning dawns, they perform it,
> because it is in their power.
> They covet fields, and seize them;
> houses, and take them away;
> they oppress householder and house,
> people and their inheritance (2:1-2).

As Micah pictures the oppressors, they are so wicked that they do not have enough time during the day to plan all of their crimes. So they lie awake at night thinking up schemes for the next day. As soon as morning breaks, they proceed to seize the property of other people, which is never supposed to leave the family according to Israelite law. Soon all are poor except themselves.

Amos reveals another effect of the rich's increase in prosperity on the needy:

> Thus says the LORD:
> For three transgressions of Israel,
> and for four, I will not revoke the punishment;
> because they sell the righteous for silver,
> and the needy for a pair of sandals (2:6).

Poor people have incurred debts because of heavy taxes and because the wealthy have cheated them. For the same reasons, they are unable to pay the debts when they come due. So the needy must sell themselves or their children into slavery, even for debts as low as the cost of a pair of sandals.[26]

Ezekiel gives a final result in 22:27, saying of Judah: "Its officials within it are like wolves tearing the prey, shedding blood, destroying lives to get dishonest gain." The rich are killing the poor. At times they do this by grasping so much of the deprived's livelihood that they starve to death. Also, the story of Ahab and Naboth's vineyard in 1 Kings 21 was probably reenacted between the wealthy and the needy in other settings. In that account Jezebel manipulates affairs so that Naboth is executed after an unjust trial and Ahab gets his property. Isaiah speaks of the same problem when he says that God:

> looked for justice, but behold, bloodshed;
> for righteousness, but behold, a cry (5:7 RSV)!

In this wordplay Yahweh looked for *mišpāṭ* (justice) but found *mišpāḥ* (bloodshed). Yahweh sought *ṣĕdāqāh* (righteousness) but heard a *ṣĕ'āqāh* (cry). The rich are giving the poor murder instead of justice.

In the midst of all this how do the wealthy view their relationship with God? Shockingly enough they think that all is well. After all their worship goes on on schedule. So Isaiah must tell them, speaking for God:

> When you come to appear before me,
> who asked this from your hand?
> Trample my courts no more;
> bringing offerings is futile;
> incense is an abomination to me.
> New moon and sabbath and calling of convocation—
> I cannot endure solemn assemblies with iniquity. . . .
> When you stretch out your hands,
> I will hide my eyes from you;
> even though you make many prayers,
> I will not listen;
> your hands are full of blood.
> Wash yourselves; make yourselves clean;
> remove the evil of your doings from before my eyes;
> cease to do evil, learn to do good;
> seek justice, rescue the oppressed,
> defend the orphan, plead for the widow (1:12-17).

The difficulty here is not that Yahweh is opposed to sacrificial worship but that God will not endure sacrifice with injustice. Judah remembers its ritual requirements and thinks that doing so maintains its relationship with Yahweh. But God sees the relationship as broken because of Judah's immorality. Yahweh will not accept their worship until they become just.

A post-exilic addition to Micah pictures the inhabitants of Judah as so uninformed that they no longer know what Yahweh requires.[27] They ask:

"With what shall I come before the LORD,
and bow myself before God on high?
Shall I come before him with burnt offerings,
with calves a year old?
Will the LORD be pleased with thousands of rams,
with ten thousands of rivers of oil?
Shall I give my firstborn for my transgression,
the fruit of my body for the sin of my soul?"
He has told you, O mortal, what is good;
and what does the LORD require of you
but to do justice, and to love kindness,
and to walk humbly with your God (6:6-8)?

In Judah's list they keep increasing the value of the possible sacrifices which they suggest. They move from ordinary burnt offerings to precious calves, to thousands of rams, to ten thousands of rivers of oil, and ultimately to human sacrifice.[28] But, as in Isaiah, Yahweh's first priority is justice. No sacrifice is acceptable without it.

## Appeals and Promises

The prophets' portrayal of Israel's social injustice, which we have just been observing, is overwhelming. At times, in response to it, the prophets appeal for justice (Isa 56:1; Hos 12:6; Amos 5:15) and make promises of a good future if Israel will be just. So Amos demands:

Let justice roll down like waters,
and righteousness like an everflowing stream (5:24).

Most creeks in Israel are so small that they dry up during the rainless summer, and only a few rivers flow all year long. Israel is to make justice as powerful as its mightiest river.

Similarly, Jeremiah promises: "For if you truly amend your ways and your doings, if you truly act justly one with another, if you do not oppress the alien, the orphan, and the widow, or shed innocent blood in this place, and if you do not go after other gods to your own hurt, then I will dwell with you in this place, in the land that I gave of old to your ancestors forever and ever" (7:5-7). It is easy to claim that one is acting justly without really doing so. But if Judah truly changes its behavior and treats the deprived with justice, then God will remain with them.

Finally, Trito-Isaiah asks:

> Is not this the fast that I choose:
> to loose the bonds of wickedness,
> to undo the thongs of the yoke,
> to let the oppressed go free,
> and to break every yoke?
> Is it not to share your bread with the hungry,
> and bring the homeless poor into your house;
> when you see the naked, to cover him,
> and not to hide yourself from your own flesh?
> Then shall your light break forth like the dawn,
> and your healing shall spring up speedily (58:6-8 RSV).

After the return from the Babylonian Exile, Israel had gone back to its old practice of observing ritual while neglecting justice. They were fasting and saw no inconsistency in oppressing the poor at the same time. However, only the wealthy have the luxury of fasting since the needy are always hungry. Fasting allows the rich to learn to wait upon God, as is characteristic of the hungry. But to fast and to mistreat the poor at the same time is doubly wicked. Those fasting are apparently learning nothing because they abuse the needy while they pretend to share their feelings.[29] So Trito-Isaiah promises blessing in the future only if the wealthy set the needy free of oppression.

### The Age to Come

In spite of appeals and promises, oppression does not end, and the poor continue to be in want. So the prophets turn to the future. If the unjust will not change their ways, God will overcome them. Yahweh will bring justice and peace on earth in a golden age to come. The hope for that age rests on the nature of God, for Yahweh is the truly just one (Isa 33:5; Zeph 3:5). Trito-Isaiah pictures God as saying: "I the LORD love justice" (61:8). And Jeremiah reports these divine words: "I am the LORD; I act with steadfast love, justice, and righteousness in the earth, for in these things I delight" (9:23 [NRSV v. 24]).

With trust in that kind of God, a post-exilic addition to Isaiah makes this promise about the age to come:[30]

> The poor (*'ănāwîm*) shall obtain fresh joy in the LORD,
> and the neediest people shall exult in the Holy One of Israel.
> For the tyrant shall be no more,
> and the scoffer shall cease to be;
> all those alert to do evil shall be cut off (29:19-20).

In the glorious age the tables will be turned. Oppressors will be destroyed, and the poor will be jubilant. Another addition to Isaiah from around the same period describes the golden age this way:[31]

> Then justice will dwell in the wilderness,
> and righteousness abide in the fruitful field.
> The effect of righteousness will be peace,
> and the result of righteousness, quietness and trust
> forever (32:16-17).

Justice will be the leading characteristic of the age to come. When there is justice, then there can be true peace and security. People will trust God, each other, and the animals, and the animals will be able to trust people and one another.[32]

A few passages connect the golden age with the ideal king, the one later Judaism calls the Messiah. Of him Isaiah says:

> A shoot shall come out from the stem[33] of Jesse,
> and a branch shall grow out of his roots.
> The spirit of the LORD shall rest on him,
> the spirit of wisdom and understanding,
> the spirit of counsel and might,
> the spirit of knowledge and the fear of the LORD.
> His delight shall be in the fear of the LORD.
> He shall not judge by what his eyes see,
> or decide by what his ears hear;
> but with righteousness he shall judge the poor,
> and decide with equity for the needy (*'ănāwê*) of the earth;
> he shall strike the earth with the rod of his mouth,
> and with the breath of his lips he shall kill the wicked.
> Righteousness shall be the belt around his waist,
> and faithfulness the belt around his loins (11:1-5).

The ideal king is going to come from the family of David's father Jesse, as the old royal line did. We saw in chapter 2 that Israel's royal ideology claimed that God's wisdom was in its rulers so that they could judge the poor justly. But reality did not correspond with the ideology since many monarchs were unrighteous. They were the heads of the establishment which oppressed the needy. So Isaiah looks for a future, ideal king who will fulfill the old ideology. Unlike the previous rulers, God's wisdom will truly be in him because he will be filled with the divine spirit. With this wisdom he will see the truth beneath appearances and be able to judge the poor fairly. He will be a truly just judge of the needy.

Developing Isaiah's idea of the branch, the ideal king, Jeremiah states:

> The days are surely coming, says the LORD, when I will raise up for David a righteous Branch, and he shall reign as king and deal wisely, and shall execute justice and righteousness in the land. In his days Judah will be saved and Israel will live in safety. And this is the name by which he will be called: "The LORD is our righteousness" (23:5-6).

This name of the future king, *Yahweh ṣidqēnû*, is a deliberate adaptation of the name of Judah's king at this time since Zedekiah means "Yahweh is righteousness."[34] Jeremiah is contrasting these two rulers by this play on their names. Zedekiah does not demonstrate the righteousness of Yahweh in his reign, but the ideal king will do the opposite. He will execute justice in the land in the age to come.

A final passage which fits with the previous two is the first servant song of Deutero-Isaiah (42:1-4). Although there is great disagreement on the identity of the Servant, I am convinced by those scholars who see a royal figure in the first song[35] and the future, ideal king in all of the servant songs.[36] The first song says:

> Here is my servant, whom I uphold,
> my chosen, in whom my soul delights;
> I have put my spirit upon him;
> he will bring forth justice to the nations. . . .
> He will not grow faint or be crushed
> until he has established justice in the earth;
> and the coastlands wait for his teaching.

As in Isaiah 11, Deutero-Isaiah states that the divine spirit will be on the coming king, and consequently, he will bring justice. All of the three texts on the ideal king studied here see him as the one who causes justice to prevail in the golden age.

At the end of this discussion of justice in the prophets, the question that needs to be answered is how it relates to the theme of this book. We have seen that the justice theme was already prevalent in the Near East and in the Israelite law codes before the prophets spoke on the topic. Some of the psalms and Wisdom literature that we shall examine in later chapters may also have treated justice before the prophets. But there is a striking change when they take up the subject. Previous treatment of justice in the Near East and the law codes does not show the fervor that the prophets do. In fact, the seriousness of some talk about justice there can be questioned. Some Near Eastern rulers may have presented themselves as champions of justice as political propaganda. For example, only the prologue and epilogue of Hammurabi's Code deal with social justice, presenting him as the fair king. The laws themselves do not treat the subject. Also, one suspects that the Israelite ideal of the just king was also often merely propaganda. While kings like Hezekiah and Josiah probably judged fairly, it is likely that others like Ahaz had the benefit of having the ideal proclaimed about them while they did not fulfill it.

In regard to Israel's law codes, the only one that was written before the prophets was the Book of the Covenant, which deals with justice but as a minor theme. Some laws in the Deuteronomic and the Holiness Codes existed in oral form before the prophets, but those codes were not written until after them. The prophets were probably the source of the high degree of justice concern in Deuteronomy.

Why were the prophets so much more fervent about justice than those before them? The fervor probably comes as a reaction to the enormity of oppression that prevailed in their time. As our Introduction stated, the paradigm this book follows is that of Wolff and Brueggemann. According to it, Israel developed new tradition when its old tradition encountered crises. The prophets had a tradition about justice from the Near East and from Israel's law codes. But the crisis of oppression of their own time produced indignation in them unlike anything in the old material. That indignation resulted in more frequent and more fervent cries for justice than had existed before.

## Notes

1. Hans Walter Wolff, *Joel and Amos,* trans. W. Janzen, S. McBride, and C. Muenchow, Hermeneia (Philadelphia: Fortress, 1977) 90–91; James Mays, *Amos, A Commentary,* OTL (Philadelphia: Westminster, 1969) 3–4.

2. Gerhard von Rad, *Old Testament Theology,* trans. D. Stalker (New York: Harper & Row, 1965) 2:136.

3. James Mays, *Micah, A Commentary,* OTL (Philadelphia: Westminster, 1976) 15.

4. Hans Walter Wolff, *Micah, A Commentary,* trans. Gary Stansell (Minneapolis: Augsburg, 1990) 6; Robert Wilson, *Prophecy and Society in Ancient Israel* (Philadelphia: Fortress, 1980) 275.

5. J. M. Ward, "Isaiah," *IDBSupp.* 457; Klaus Koch, *The Prophets,* trans. Margaret Kohl (Philadelphia: Fortress, 1982) 1:106.

6. Von Rad, *Old Testament Theology,* 2:147; Wilson, *Prophecy and Society,* 271; Joseph Blenkinsopp, *A History of Prophecy in Israel* (Philadelphia: Westminster, 1983) 115.

7. Norman Gottwald, *The Hebrew Bible—A Socio-Literary Introduction* (Philadelphia: Fortress, 1985) 403–4; Blenkinsopp, *History of Prophecy,* 166.

8. Koch, *The Prophets,* 2:17.

9. Wolff, *Joel and Amos,* 205.

10. Wolff, *Micah,* 97–98.

11. Ibid., 99.

12. J.J.M. Roberts, *Nahum, Habakkuk, and Zephaniah, A Commentary,* OTL (Louisville: Westminster, 1991) 89.

13. Mays, *Amos,* 144.

14. Ibid.

15. Wolff, *Joel and Amos,* 327.

16. Otto Kaiser, *Isaiah 1–12, A Commentary,* trans. John Bowden, OTL, 2nd ed. (Philadelphia: Westminster, 1983) 227.

17. Otto Kaiser, *Isaiah 13–39. A Commentary,* trans. R. A. Wilson, OTL (Philadelphia: Westminster, 1974) 278.

18. Roberts, *Nahum, Habakkuk,* 213.

19. David Petersen, *Haggai and Zechariah 1–8, A Commentary*, OTL (Philadelphia: Westminster, 1984) 290.

20. William Holladay, *Jeremiah 1*, Hermeneia (Philadelphia: Fortress, 1986) 594.

21. Walther Eichrodt, *Ezekiel, A Commentary*, trans. Cosslett Quin, OTL (Philadelphia: Westminster, 1970) 214.

22. Kaiser, *Isaiah 13–39*, 320.

23. Wolff, *Joel and Amos*, 201–2.

24. Mays, *Amos*, 116.

25. Wolff, *Joel and Amos*, 276.

26. Ibid., 165.

27. Wolff, *Micah*, 172.

28. Ibid., 178.

29. Leslie Hoppe, "Isaiah 58:1-12, Fasting and Idolatry," *BTB* 13 (1983) 45.

30. Kaiser, *Isaiah 13–39*, 278.

31. Ibid., 333.

32. Ibid., 335.

33. R.B.Y. Scott, "The Book of Isaiah, Chapters 1–39," *The Interpreter's Bible*, ed. George Buttrick and others (Nashville: Abingdon, 1956) 5:248.

34. Holladay, *Jeremiah 1*, 617, 619.

35. Claus Westermann, *Isaiah 40–66, A Commentary*, trans. David Stalker, OTL (Philadelphia: Westminster, 1969) 94; Blenkinsopp, *History of Prophecy*, 215–16.

36. Helmer Ringgren, *The Messiah in the Old Testament*, Studies in Biblical Theology 18 (London: SCM Press, 1956).

# 5

# *The Psalms*

## *Social Setting*

This chapter treats frequent passages on social justice in the psalms. It is likely that the authors of most of the psalms were members of the guilds of singers who worked at the Jerusalem Temple. Guilds such as the sons of Asaph and the sons of Korah are referred to in the headings of various psalms. Lay people came to the Temple to recite individual laments and thanksgivings. The oppressed were among them, and so, the psalmists got to know them when they brought their problems as the subject for prayer. We do not know the social status of the psalmists, but if they were not among the deprived themselves, at least, they wrote from the viewpoint of the oppressed they encountered.[1]

In the pre-exilic period the Temple personnel were in a difficult position because the Temple was under the domination of the rulers. They were the very ones who permitted their subordinates to oppress the poor. But, as we have seen in previous chapters, the royal ideology claimed that the sovereign was just. So the Temple personnel had some basis for supporting the oppressed in the cult.[2]

In the post-exilic era some members of the Wisdom movement became psalmists and wrote a few private, Wisdom psalms, which were not used in the cult.[3] It is likely that they were people of wealth. So when they support the deprived, they are opposing many members of their own class, as some of the prophets did.

## Social Injustice

Some passages in the psalms describe the social injustice that exists in Israel. In a few texts the psalmists imagine the motives and thoughts which influence oppressors. Psalm 10 says that they are greedy (v. 3) and then proceeds to describe what goes through their minds:

> In the pride of their countenance the wicked say,
> "God will not seek it out";
> all their thoughts are, "There is no God."
> Their ways prosper at all times;
> your judgments are on high, out of their sight;
> as for their foes, they scoff at them.
> They think in their heart, "We shall not be moved;
> throughout all generations we shall not meet adversity"
> (vv. 4-6).

The oppressors are confident because their lives are going well, and they only experience success. They conclude that there is no retribution, either because there is no God or because God does not repay people for evil. So they anticipate continued prosperity in the future. As Walter Brueggemann points out, they live in the usual mode of social relations. They believe that there are only two parties involved in these relations, themselves and the weak. They dismiss the third party, God, as an effective player in social interaction.[4]

Psalm 49 states that another motive of the rich is trust in their wealth (v. 7 [NRSV v. 6]). But the psalmist is consoled with this advice:

> Do not be afraid when some become rich,
> when the wealth of their houses increases.
> For when they die they will carry nothing away;
> their wealth will not go down after them
> (vv. 17-18 [NRSV vv. 16-17]).

Rich oppressors must leave their wealth to others at death (v. 11 [NRSV v. 10]). Although most Wisdom psalms were probably written by the affluent, this one seems to come from the circle of the poor.[5] This deprived person understands a motive of the wealthy but sees how superficial it is.

When the psalmists move from oppressors' motivation to their actions, these writers are seldom specific. Psalm 15:5 is an exception. It is part of an entrance liturgy in which worshippers ask priests what kind of people may enter the Temple area.[6] Part of the priests' response is

> Those . . . who do not lend money at interest,
> and do not take a bribe against the innocent.

We have seen interest forbidden before in the law codes and Ezekiel. And bribery was outlawed in every source examined so far, Near Eastern documents, Israelite law codes, and the prophetic writings.

Like the prophets, other passages talk about oppressors killing the needy. Psalm 94:5-6 says:

> They crush your people, O LORD,
> and afflict your heritage.
> They kill the widow and the stranger,
> they murder the orphan.

This is a post-exilic psalm with Wisdom elements in it. The evil-doers probably come from the leadership of the people and kill the deprived through dishonest legal proceedings. Verses 20-21 mention wicked rulers who condemn the innocent to death.[7]

Similarly, Psalm 10:8-10 says of the oppressors:

> They sit in ambush in the villages;
> in hiding places they murder the innocent.
> Their eyes stealthily watch for the helpless;
> they lurk in secret like a lion in its covert;
> they lurk that they may seize the poor;
> they seize the poor and drag them off in their net.
> They stoop, they crouch,
> and the helpless fall by their might.

It is possible that this description is meant literally and that the wealthy have sent underlings to murder poor people so that the rich may get their property. It is also possible that the passage is figurative and refers to killing the needy through unjust legal proceedings and by depriving them of their livelihood.

Because of this kind of oppression by the affluent, some psalmists cry out to God for help. The author of Psalm 10 reacts to the threat just described with the words:

> Rise up, O LORD; O God, lift up your hand;
> do not forget the oppressed. . . .
> Break the arm of the wicked and evildoers;
> seek out their wickedness until you find none (vv. 12, 15).

Since the deprived are helpless, the psalmist appeals to God as their one reliable source of aid. The author asks that Yahweh overpower the oppressors and rescue the poor.

Some psalmists identify with the needy and call upon God to save them from powerful enemies. One says:

> Incline your ear, O LORD, and answer me,
> for I am poor and needy (86:1).

Another cries out:

> I am poor and needy;
> hasten to me, O God!
> You are my help and my deliverer;
> O LORD, do not delay (70:6 [NRSV v. 5])!

## Human Helpers of the Poor

However, Yahweh does not always help the deprived directly since God can aid them at times through other people. One psalm, 72, returns to the theme of the ruler as the deliverer of the poor. This psalm was probably used at the enthronement of a king or at a royal festival during the reign of a monarch.[8] It begins with a prayer of the congregation for him:

> Give the king your justice, O God,
> and your righteousness to a king's son.
> May he judge your people with righteousness,
> and your poor with justice. . . .
> May he defend the cause of the poor of the people,
> give deliverance to the needy,
> and crush the oppressor (vv. 1-4).

Since the ruler is the highest judge in the land and judging is a key role for monarchs, this king requires divine assistance for this task. This prayer acknowledges the existence of oppression in the country and asks that the king may have divine justice to oppose it and fairly judge the poor.

Later, this psalm returns to this theme and says of the king:

> He delivers the needy when they call,
> the poor and those who have no helper.
> He has pity on the weak and the needy,
> and saves the lives of the needy.
> From oppression and violence he redeems their life;
> and precious is their blood in his sight (vv. 12-14).

This is no longer a prayer that the king may have the justice of God but a confident affirmation that he already has it. We have returned here to the royal ideology that the ruler is the just judge of the poor, who rescues them from oppressors.

When the psalms turn to ordinary people's dealings with the needy, their statements are rather bland. Their few comments about helping the poor all come from late, post-exilic psalms, and they sound as if there is no justice crisis when they are written. First, Psalm 112 states:

> It is well with those who deal generously and lend,
> who conduct their affairs with justice. . . .
> They have distributed freely, they have given to the
> poor (vv. 5, 9).

The closest we come to a justice concern here is the line which mentions conducting affairs with justice. But it probably merely means taking care of business affairs with integrity, including not charging interest and acting without deceit.[9] The other parts of the verses only refer to loans and gifts to the poor.

Psalm 37 merely mentions the last concerns. Verse 21 is about charity ("The righteous are generous and keep giving"), and verse 26 deals with loans, saying that the righteous "are ever giving liberally and lending." Psalm 41 is even more vague, only stating that one who deals prudently with the poor is happy (v. 2 [NRSV v. 1]). By dealing prudently it probably means looking after the needy.[10]

*God Helps the Poor*

Although the psalms say little about human assistance for the deprived, they mention divine help more often than any other topic in the area of social justice. Psalm 82 contrasts Yahweh with the other gods in this respect in an imaginative way. It begins:

> God has taken his place in the divine council;
> in the midst of the gods he holds judgment:
> "How long will you judge unjustly
> and show partiality to the wicked?
> Give justice to the weak and the orphan;
> maintain the right of the lowly and the destitute.
> Rescue the weak and the needy;
> deliver them from the hand of the wicked" (vv. 1-4).

Israel believed that there was an assembly of the gods in the heavens and that Yahweh was the king of the council. Yahweh had the real power, and the others were God's subordinates. In this text Yahweh is placing the gods on trial because they have not delivered the poor from oppression. We saw in chapter 1 that the Near East in general believed that justice for the needy originated with the gods. But they have not been doing their duty, and so, later in the psalm Yahweh condemns them and takes over the role of protector of the poor for the whole earth. This psalm expresses the belief that Yahweh is the only God who truly delivers the needy.

Likewise, Psalm 99:4 calls Yahweh the "lover of justice," and 68:6 (NRSV v. 5) says that God is the "father of orphans and protector of widows." In addition, Yahweh feeds the hungry according to Psalm 132. It states that Zion is God's eternal residence, and the consequence of Yahweh's presence is that God abundantly blesses its provisions and satisfies its poor with bread (v. 15).[11]

Psalm 146 contrasts Yahweh and rulers in their care for the needy. This is a late psalm, written after Israel's many bad experiences with monarchs. So verse 3 tells readers not to put their trust in princes. The old ideology of the just ruler has not proven true since monarchs have treated the poor unfairly. Rather, Yahweh is the true protector of the weak, and thus, Yahweh's

name appears five times at the beginning of lines in verses 7-9 of
the Hebrew text. In translation they say that Yahweh is the one

> who executes justice for the oppressed;
> who gives food to the hungry.
> The LORD sets the prisoners free;
> the LORD opens the eyes of the blind.
> The LORD lifts up those who are bowed down;
> the LORD loves the righteous.
> The LORD watches over the strangers;
> he upholds the orphan and the widow.

Unlike rulers, Yahweh truly gives justice to the oppressed and re-
lieves sojourners, orphans, and widows. God is the real ruler, and
so, the last verse of the psalm states that "The LORD will reign
forever."

Psalms 9 and 10, which originally constituted a single psalm,[12]
give a similar picture of God. They say that Yahweh "does not
forget the cry of the poor *('ǎnāwîm)*" (9:13 [NRSV v. 12]).
After describing actions of the oppressors, Psalm 10 states:

> But you do see! Indeed you note trouble and grief,
> that you may take it into your hands;
> the helpless commit themselves to you;
> you have been the helper of the orphan. . . .
> O LORD, you will hear the desire of the poor *('ǎnāwîm)*;
> you will strengthen their heart,
> you will incline your ear
> to do justice for the orphan and the oppressed (vv. 14, 17-18).

The psalmist is convinced that God does care about the oppression of the weak and is the one who will give them real justice.
Walter Brueggemann calls Psalms 9 and 10 an extraordinary act
of counter-speech. They quote the words of the oppressors and
then proceed to mock and override them. Thus, these psalms
constitute social inversion and even social control for those who
are usually powerless.[13] At least, when they recite these psalms,
they see Yahweh in charge of life, rather than the rich. Then
there is finally the possibility of deliverance.

Like the prophets, the psalmists add to Israel's legacy of social justice thought. The conditions of social injustice which they

describe and their appeals for help show that they write for people who are enduring crises like those which the prophets' poor contemporaries faced. Again, crises produce new thought. The psalmists react to them by adding to past tradition new expressions of confidence in the willingness and ability of God to help the oppressed.

## Notes

1. Sigmund Mowinckel, *The Psalms in Israel's Worship,* trans. D. R. Ap-Thomas (Nashville: Abingdon, 1962) 2:85, 92.

2. Norman Gottwald, *The Hebrew Bible—A Socio-Literary Introduction* (Philadelphia: Fortress, 1985) 540.

3. Mowinckel, *Psalms in Worship,* 2:106.

4. Walter Brueggemann, "Psalms 9–10: A Counter to Conventional Social Reality," *The Bible and the Politics of Exegesis,* ed. David Jobling and others (Cleveland: Pilgrim, 1991) 8–10.

5. Hans-Joachim Kraus, *Psalms 1–59, A Commentary,* trans. Hilton Oswald (Minneapolis: Augsburg, 1988) 480–81.

6. Ibid., 226–27.

7. Ibid., 239–40; A. A. Anderson, *The Book of Psalms,* New Century Bible (London: Oliphants, 1972) 2:672.

8. Hans-Joachim Kraus, *Psalms 60–150, A Commentary,* trans. Hilton Oswald (Minneapolis: Augsburg, 1989) 76.

9. Ibid., 364.

10. Kraus, *Psalms 1–59,* 431.

11. Anderson, *Book of Psalms,* 2:884.

12. Kraus, *Psalms 1–59,* 191.

13. Brueggemann, "Psalms 9–10," 11.

# 6

# *Late Narrative Works*

## *The Deuteronomic History*

Compared to the rest of the Hebrew Bible, there are surprisingly few references to social justice in the narrative books. All of them that contain such items were written in their final form relatively late. The earliest of them and the work with the most references is the Deuteronomic History. It consists of Joshua, Judges, 1 and 2 Samuel, and 1 and 2 Kings, with the earlier Book of Deuteronomy placed at the beginning as a preface. Although the Deuteronomic History contains earlier sources, its first form was probably written shortly before the Babylonian Exile, and its final version likely was created during the Exile.

The first mention of social justice in the Deuteronomic History occurs in the song of Hannah (1 Sam 2:1-10). This song was not originally connected with Hannah's situation but has been inserted into the story at this point by someone who felt that it was appropriate. It was composed during the monarchic period.[1] The relevant lines are

> The bows of the mighty are broken,
> but the feeble gird on strength.
> Those who were full have hired themselves out for bread,
> but those who were hungry have ceased to hunger forever. . . .[2]
> The LORD makes poor and makes rich;
> he brings low, he also exalts.
> He raises up the poor from the dust;

he lifts the needy from the ash heap,
to make them sit with princes
and inherit a seat of honor (vv. 4-8).

This song contains the same kind of social inversion that we saw in Psalms 9–10. The author who lives during the oppressive period of the monarchy visualizes a different kind of world in which the roles of the rich and poor are reversed. There the rich are poverty-stricken while the needy leave the ash heap of the town dump, where they sleep and beg for alms, to sit on thrones.[3] This writer can talk like this because of faith that Yahweh will make this decisive change.

The next relevant texts deal with the contrast between Samuel and his sons. 1 Samuel 8:3 says that Samuel's "sons did not follow in his ways, but turned aside after gain; they took bribes and perverted justice." On the contrary, at the end of his career Samuel asks Israel: "Whom have I oppressed *('āšaqtî)*? Whom have I crushed *(raṣṣôtî)*? Or from whose hand have I taken a bribe to blind my eyes with it?" They answer: "You have not oppressed us or crushed us or taken anything from the hand of anyone" (12:3-4). Samuel has been a just judge, not taking bribes or oppressing the innocent. He is a model for the time of the Deuteronomic History when too many judges are like his sons.

The third passage dealing with social justice is Nathan's parable to David (2 Sam 12:1-4). It reads:

> There were two men in a certain city, the one rich and the other poor. The rich man had very many flocks and herds; but the poor man had nothing but one little ewe lamb, which he had bought. He brought it up, and it grew up with him and with his children; it used to eat of his meager fare, and drink from his cup, and lie in his bosom, and it was like a daughter to him. Now there came a traveler to the rich man, and he was loath to take one of his own flock or herd to prepare for the wayfarer who had come to him, but he took the poor man's lamb, and prepared that for the guest who had come to him.

Nathan tells the story in order to get David to indict himself for his adultery with Bathsheba and murder of her husband Uriah. But the parable itself is a story of social injustice. The rich man abuses his power by forcing the poor man to give up his pet for the wealthy man's gain. David's sin also involved similar abuse. His role as king was to protect the weak, but instead he used his power to oppress and eliminate Uriah.[4]

The next narrative, 1 Kings 17:8-16, is an example of charity toward a poor person. Elijah is hungry and asks another needy person, a widow, for food. She objects that she has almost nothing to give him, but he assures her that her food will miraculously be multiplied if she helps him. She believes the prediction and feeds him, and the promise is fulfilled. When its first hearers heard this legend, one thing that they learned from it was a lesson in charity. The widow is a model of sharing with the poor, even if one has little to give.

The most striking story of social injustice in the narrative books is the account of Naboth's vineyard (1 Kgs 21). Here King Ahab of Israel covets this vineyard that is next to his palace. When he offers to buy it, Naboth must refuse because Israelite law forbids selling ancestral property. When Ahab acts moody because of his failure, his wife Jezebel offers to solve the problem for him. She arranges matters so that two false witnesses bring testimony against Naboth at a public gathering. They accuse him of cursing God and the king, and the community executes Naboth for this crime by stoning. Then Ahab proceeds to take possession of his vineyard. This story is a good example of social injustice in the monarchic period. The powerful seize the property of the lower class by dishonest means like false witness in legal proceedings. At times, the oppressors even resort to murder to gain what they want.

## The Book of Ruth

The Book of Ruth is a story from the fifth or fourth centuries B.C.E. In it Boaz is portrayed as a righteous man who cares for Ruth, a needy widow and sojourner. Boaz is introduced to the story as a mighty man of wealth (2:1). By divine providence Ruth comes to his field to glean or pick up the scraps left by the reapers, as Israelite law permits the poor to do. When Boaz learns that Ruth is doing this, he tells her to continue to glean in his field and offers her water when she gets thirsty. She acknowledges that his care is extraordinary considering that she is a foreigner and not one of his servants (vv. 10, 13). At mealtime Boaz offers Ruth food and drink, and when she returns to work, he instructs his reapers to let her glean even among the standing sheaves and to intentionally drop sheaves for her to gather.

Why does Boaz do these kind deeds? He is responding to Ruth's good deeds to Naomi (2:11), and he is probably attracted to Ruth, but the author is also picturing him as one who properly cares for the poor. Ruth is an archetypal needy person being poor, a widow, and a sojourner. Boaz reacts to her need by keeping the gleaning laws and going beyond this by making gleaning easy for her and giving her food and drink.

## The Chronicler

The Deuteronomic History is the first major history of Israel, and the work of the Chronicler is the second, covering some of the same material as the previous history. The Chronicler redacted 1 and 2 Chronicles and probably also Ezra and Nehemiah although scholars are divided on whether the latter books should be included. The Chronicler wrote between 400 and 300 B.C.E.

In the Chronicler's first reference to justice (2 Chr 19:5-7), he reports that when King Jehoshaphat appointed judges for the cities of Judah, he instructed them:

> Consider what you are doing, for you judge not on behalf of human beings but on the LORD's behalf; he is with you in giving judgment. Now let the fear of the LORD be upon you; take care what you do, for there is no perversion of justice with the LORD our God, or partiality, or taking of bribes.

In this late work the perennial Near Eastern and Israelite concerns for fair judgment and the avoidance of partiality and bribes appear again.

The other pertinent passage is in a section where the Chronicler is using the memoirs of Nehemiah (Neh 5:1-13). There Nehemiah relates an episode of injustice which took place during his governorship of Judah. Some of the lower class reported that they had taken loans from the wealthy because of the hardship caused by famine. The rich had broken Israelite law by keeping pledges from the others and possibly by taking interest from them. The latter is unclear because some scholars translate verses 7, 10-11 with terms for interest,[5] but others say that these verses still deal with taking pledges.[6] Regardless, the wealthy have forced the lower class to surrender some of their property to them and to enslave their children to pay their debts. Nehemiah confronts the rich about their injustice and forces them to return the others' property and the profit they have made on them. Even the experience of the Babylonian Exile has not made an impact on these offenders since they continue to treat the lower class in the same way that the wealthy before the Exile did. But Nehemiah is an example of a just official who takes the part of the oppressed.

While the narrative books have few texts dealing with social justice, the ones which are present have the same care for this topic as the law codes, prophets, and psalms. Social justice remains a matter of deep concern.

## Notes

1. Ralph Klein, *1 Samuel*, Word Biblical Commentary 10 (Waco: Word Books, 1983) 15.

2. Hans Hertzberg, *I & II Samuel, A Commentary*, trans. J. S. Bowden, OTL (Philadelphia: Westminster, 1964) 27.

3. Klein, *1 Samuel*, 18.

4. J. Emmette Weir, "The Poor are Powerless: A Response to R. J. Coggins," *Exp Tim* 100 (1988) 13.

5. NRSV, RSV, NAB.

6. NJB; REB; Jacob Myers, *Ezra, Nehemiah*, AB 14 (Garden City: Doubleday, 1965) 128–29; Joseph Blenkinsopp, *Ezra-Nehemiah, A Commentary*, OTL (Philadelphia: Westminster, 1988) 259.

# 7

# *The Wisdom Literature*[1]

The Wisdom literature consists of the books of Proverbs, Job, Ecclesiastes, Sirach, and Wisdom. The latter two are considered apocryphal by Jews and Protestants, but we shall include them in this chapter since they are an integral part of Wisdom literature, regardless of their canonicity. The five Wisdom books refer rather frequently to social justice. Do these references add new perspectives to the biblical treatment of this theme? The former view of Wisdom minimized the value of Wisdom's contributions to such a topic since, according to this view, old Wisdom in Israel was consistently secular. It later became religious and ethical through the influence of Israel's faith.[2] Thus, according to this perspective, social justice was not an indigenous theme of Wisdom. Wisdom adopted it at a late period under the influence of prophecy.

Today the former view of Wisdom is seen to be decreasingly adequate. A number of authors have shown that it is impossible to separate religion and ethics from Wisdom at any stage of its development. Wisdom in Israel always had some religious assumptions. And it is natural that this should be so since the earlier Wisdom literature of the rest of the Near East was also consistently religious.[3] Since Israel's Wisdom contained religious elements from the beginning, it is possible that it also always had a concern with social justice. In that case the theme was not borrowed from prophecy in the oldest parts of the Book of Proverbs since they antedate the written prophets. That early Wisdom literature received its concepts of justice from Near Eastern sources and specifically at times from other Near Eastern Wisdom literature,[4] some of which we surveyed in chapter 1. The later Israelite Wisdom writings were produced after some of the prophetic books and may have been influenced by prophecy.

## Social Class of the Wise

As in prior chapters, we shall now examine the part of Israelite society that produced the Wisdom literature and its intended audience. Any part of Israelite society may have coined individual Wisdom sayings which later were incorporated into Wisdom books, but those books reveal a narrower social setting for their origin and use. It is generally believed that the books were produced and read by people with wealth. It is very likely that the earliest collections of proverbs were assembled in the royal court. The court probably contained a school for the training of courtiers and scribes who worked there, and the collections were used in that school. There are various reasons for accepting the court-school origin of proverb collections: First, Egyptian and Mesopotamian Wisdom writings were produced in court schools. Second, the biblical Wisdom books have forms, terminology, and a world view different from the rest of the Hebrew Bible. Thus, Wisdom materials were written in a different social setting, and the court would be a logical possibility. Third, there would have been a need in Israel for a court school since the court employed professionals who required specialized training. And finally, the Wisdom literature contains numerous sayings about the king and court.

After the destruction of the monarchy, the Wisdom movement continued and produced the Wisdom books as they are today. Those books show that the movement remained among people with wealth, there being many signs of this in the material. It places a priority on attitudes that correspond to that setting. Ostentation and loudness are shunned, but taste, elegance, self-control, and propriety are appreciated. The authors are conservative, satisfied with the status quo and opposed to change. Thus, there is great respect for authority (Prov 14:35; 16:10). The books have an international character, and wealth is required to make such contacts. Many sayings presuppose that the authors possess abundance (Job 31; Prov 21:14; Eccl 2:18-23). Ben Sira tells more about his personal life than other wisdom writers, and what he says reveals his affluence. He has travelled widely (34:9-12), and he conducts a school and charges a large tuition (51:23, 28). He gives copious advice about behavior at banquets (31:12–32:13) and treatment of servants (33:24-31). This kind of evidence leads many scholars to conclude that Wisdom comes from an upper-class setting and that people with wealth have produced the Wisdom corpus.[5]

## *Attitudes Toward Wealth*

Some of the attitudes toward wealth in these writings are what one would expect from affluent people. For one thing, they have respect for the power of money. Ecclesiastes 10:19 says that "money answers everything" (RSV). According to Proverbs 22:7, the rich rule the poor, so the poor must grovel while the rich can choose to be rude (18:23). Wealth is a rich person's protection (10:15) and brings honor (10:30-31). The rich are surrounded by friends while the poor are isolated (14:20; 19:4; Sir 13:21-22).

Second, the wise occasionally express the opinion that people should enjoy their abundance. According to Qoheleth, the author of Ecclesiastes, it is God who gives the power to enjoy wealth (5:18-19). Ben Sira says:

> My child, treat yourself well, according to your means,
> and present worthy offerings to the Lord.
> Remember that death does not tarry,
> and the decree of Hades has not been shown to you.
> Do good to friends before you die,
> and reach out and give to them as much as you can.
> Do not deprive yourself of a day's enjoyment;
> do not let your share of desired good pass by you.
> Will you not leave the fruit of your labors to another,
> and what you acquired by toil to be divided by lot?
> Give, and take, and indulge yourself,
> because in Hades one cannot look for luxury (14:11-16).

Commentators generally conclude that the command to do good and give to a friend in verse 13 refers to hospitality and not to charity.[6] With this understanding of verse 13, almost the entire passage advises people in a variety of ways to enjoy wealth while life remains.

Finally, the retribution theory, that people get what they deserve, is a basic theme in Wisdom. This is a congenial theory for the wealthy. They have a right to their affluence because they have earned it through hard work and a moral life. So the Wisdom writings contain the thought that the rich are the good. Job is the epitome of this equation before his misfortunes. In the same vein the wise conclude that wealth comes from wisdom (Prov 3:16) and that it is the wise who keep their wealth (21:20). Likewise, diligence produces riches, and laziness leads to poverty (10:4). All of the above attitudes are self-serving for the affluent and the sort of self-protective thoughts that one would expect a social class to have.

What is then so striking about the Wisdom literature is that although these attitudes exist, they are in the minority. In fact, the wise express many opinions that move in the opposite direction. For one thing, they are very aware of the limits of wealth's power. They mention various items which are of greater value than riches: wisdom (Prov 3:13-15), quiet (17:1), a good name (22:1), and health (Sir 30:14-16). And particularly the fear of Yahweh and love excel wealth (Prov 15:16-17).

The wise also note problems with riches. They provide no assistance on the day of wrath (11:4), and they are here today and gone tomorrow (23:4-5). Ben Sira observes that the rich and poor can suddenly exchange positions (18:25-26). Also, sin and riches lie close together, and it requires great care to gain wealth and avoid wrong (27:1-3). And particularly Qoheleth expands in great detail on the worthlessness of riches (2:4-11; 5:9-16). He speaks repeatedly about the vanity of amassing wealth and leaving it to heirs (2:18-21; 6:1-3). And if the rich equated themselves with the good on the basis of the retribution theory, Qoheleth undermines this confidence completely by denying the validity of the theory (8:10-14).

Furthermore, the Wisdom literature contains a statement that trust in wealth is wrong (Job 31:24-25, 28), and one of the wise asks to be neither rich nor poor and thus avoid the problems of both conditions (Prov 30:7-9). The statements above show that while the wise appreciated their wealth at times, there are many other instances in which they saw the limits of affluence's worth.

## Charity

With this ambivalent attitude toward their wealth, what kind of attitudes did the wise have toward the poor and what kind of actions toward the needy did they advocate? They advise two major approaches to the poor. First, like the Near East generally, the Israelite law codes, the psalms, and rarely the prophets, the sages recommend charity or gifts. At times they comment negatively about those who do not share with the helpless. Eliphaz wrongly accuses Job of not giving the hungry and thirsty bread and water (Job 22:7). Proverbs 28:27 contrasts giving to the poor with raising one's eyes. It predicts a great curse for those who raise their eyes to avoid seeing those in need. Ben Sira warns against angering poor people by making them wait for a gift and against not giving to the needy (4:1-5).

On the other hand, there are numerous passages that speak positively about charity. For example, Proverbs 22:9 promises blessing for those with a "good" eye who give from their bread to the poor. Unlike those who raise their eyes in 28:27, those with a "good" eye see and respond to need. 11:24 talks about one who scatters and yet grows richer. "Scattering" probably refers to giving to the deprived, as it does in Psalm 112:9.[7] Especially Job discusses this subject in chapter 31, his final oath in which he swears that he has not offended in any of the ways that he mentions. Donations to the needy are a major topic in the oath. He says that he would deserve punishment

> If I have withheld anything that the poor desired,
> or have caused the eyes of the widow to fail,
> or have eaten my morsel alone,
> and the orphan has not eaten from it—
> for from my youth I reared the orphan like a father,
> and from my mother's womb I guided the widow—
> if I have seen anyone perish for lack of clothing,
> or a poor person without covering,
> whose loins have not blessed me,
> and who was not warmed with the fleece of my sheep
> (vv. 16-20).

Job is saying that he has not withheld anything that the poor desired, even when their demands were immoderate. He has not caused widows' eyes to fail; their sight has not been blurred through weeping over their scarcity. On the contrary, throughout his life he has acted like a father to the fatherless and widows and fed them. Furthermore, Job has clothed every poor person in sight. This is a strong statement by one of the wise on the moral necessity of charity to the poor.

Ben Sira regularly uses the word "alms" for this necessary donation to the needy. One instance is 12:3, in which he says that no good will come to one who does not give alms. Ben Sira urges his readers to not make the lowly wait for alms and to store up almsgiving in their treasuries (29:8, 12). Alms was not an early term in the Hebrew Bible for gifts to the poor, but Ben Sira follows a common, later Jewish practice in using the word.[8] However, charity to the needy was a common Wisdom mandate both when the word "alms" was used for it and when it was not.

Ben Sira's treatment of the subject of loans and surety is similar in part to the wise's attitude toward charity. He begins discussing loans by recommending that his readers give loans to those in need out of mercy (29:1-2). Likewise, he advises being surety, offering collateral, for a neighbor (vv. 14, 20). This advice goes against the Wisdom tradition, for the wise consistently warned against the dangers of surety on the basis of good, business sense (Prov 6:1-5). And Ben Sira is too much a part of his tradition not to heed that caution, for he himself warns against the pitfalls involved in surety in 29:15-20. Also, he notes the problems with giving loans in vv. 3-7. But it is not remarkable that Ben Sira gives this negative, practical advice. Then he follows the tradition of the past. What is remarkable is his positive statements on the matter. They show that his concern for the needy sometimes overcomes his practical sense. Then he is willing to take risks, offering money to the poor with a chance of loss. This is similar to giving to them.

## Social Justice

The wise's second major approach to the needy is giving them justice. First, the wise describe the problem of injustice that exists. Proverbs 30:13-14 depicts the proud who devour the needy like cannibals. Wisdom 2:10-11 portrays the ungodly planning to oppress the poor and widow and claiming that might makes right. In addition to such general descriptions, the wise also mention the specific ways in which the poor are cheated which we have seen often before. Numerous passages refer to the problem of false weights (Prov 11:1; 16:11; 20:10, 23; Sir 42:4). Also some texts talk about moving landmarks (Job 24:2; Prov 15:25; 22:28). Proverbs 23:10, for instance, commands the reader not to move a landmark and thus enter the fields of the fatherless. The misuse of pledges reappears when Eliphaz falsely accuses Job by saying

> You have exacted pledges from your family for no reason,
> and stripped the naked of their clothing (22:6).

Job supposedly took the poor's clothing as collateral and gave them no loan in return. As we have seen, Israelite law demanded that clothing not be kept as a pledge overnight, but Job is accused of keeping the garments permanently. Finally, the issue of taking interest from fellow Israelites comes up again when Proverbs 28:8 predicts the loss of wealth gained in this way.

As in the sources previously studied here, the method of cheating the poor that the wise mention most often is injustice in the law court. Proverbs 22:22 commands:

> Do not rob the poor because they are poor,
> or crush the afflicted at the gate.

This text forbids giving the poor injustice in trials because they lack the prestige and financial resources of the rich. Other texts refer to the specific ways that the rich used their advantages to deprive the poor of justice that we have seen before. Some passages warn against partiality of judges (Prov 24:23-26; 28:21; Sir 7:6), and many statements note that judges were partial toward the rich because of bribes (Prov 15:27; 17:8, 23; Eccl 7:7). Another unjust practice frequently decried is false witnessing (Prov 19:5, 9, 28; 21:28; 24:28).

Some Wisdom writings, next, spell out the consequences of all of the above unjust acts toward the needy. The poor endure the labor of producing food only to lose it through injustice and go hungry (Prov 13:23). The wicked seize the homes of the poor (Job 20:19), and the rich take violent possession of the land of the widows and fatherless (22:8-9). Naked and homeless, the deprived live in the open without shelter (24:2-11) and cry out in anguish to God (34:28; 35:9).

Among the Wisdom writers, the smallest response to all of this suffering is Qoheleth's. He reports that he has seen the strong oppress the weak, but all that he can say in reaction is that it is better to be dead than alive (4:1-2). In 5:7 he says that it is not surprising that the poor are treated unjustly since each unjust official is treated unfairly by one above him.[9] Apparently Qoheleth does not see any hope in trying to overcome injustice. This is typical of him because he does not see much hope in life generally. However, even Qoheleth is not unmoved by injustice.[10] He sympathizes but is immobilized by his despair.

On the other hand, most of the other Wisdom books call for a more active response to the problem. The Book of Proverbs begins with a statement of its purpose. Included is the aim that readers will know "righteousness *(ṣedeq),* justice *(mišpāṭ),* and equity *(mêšārîm)*" (1:3). Certainly *mišpāṭ* means justice and is so translated in most modern versions at this place.[11] As we saw in chapter 2, *ṣedeq* also often has the connotation of justice and probably has it here. The same may be true of *mêšārîm* which the NJB correspondingly translates as "fair dealing." Thus, at least one and perhaps as many as three of the words in Proverbs 1:3 indicate that the editors regard instruction in justice as a primary purpose of their book.

Minimally showing justice to the poor means not maltreating them as others do. In Job's final oath he swears that this has been true of him:

> If I have raised my hand against the orphan,
> because I saw I had supporters at the gate;
> then let my shoulder blade fall from my shoulder,
> and let my arm be broken from its socket (31:21-22).

If he had previously cheated the fatherless, Job could count on his influence with the town elders. And so, the victim could not have brought a successful charge against him in court. But Job has not used his advantage so unfairly.

However, the counsel of the wise goes beyond not doing wrong. It also calls for the active doing of right. Some passages advocate the just judgment of the poor (Prov 29:7), many of them mentioning the ruler's responsibility in this regard. Proverbs 29:14 says:

> If a king judges the poor with equity
> his throne will be established for ever.

And in 31:9, the king is told to judge righteously and to maintain the rights of the poor. To non-royal judges, Sirach 4:8-9 says:

> Give a hearing to the poor,
> and return their greeting politely.
> Rescue the oppressed from the oppressor;
> and do not be hesitant in giving a verdict.

Thus, Ben Sira tells his readers to judge fairly. If they have the influential position of judges, they are to use it to rescue the poor from those who would rob them in court.

The strongest statement on social justice in the Wisdom literature is Job 29:11-17. Here Job describes his behavior before his misfortunes struck. This description is the author's concept of an ideal person:

> When the ear heard, it commended me,
> and when the eye saw, it approved;
> because I delivered the poor who cried,
> and the orphan who had no helper.
> The blessing of the wretched came upon me,
> and I caused the widow's heart to sing for joy.
> I put on righteousness, and it was clothed with me;[12]
> my justice was like a robe and a turban.
> I was eyes to the blind,
> and feet to the lame.
> I was a father to the needy,
> and I championed the cause of the stranger.
> I broke the fangs of the unrighteous,
> and made them drop their prey from their teeth.

According to verse 14, Job put on justice like garments. But more than that, justice also put on Job like a garment; that is,

Job was the incarnation of justice. Ideal people are totally just, so they rescue the poor, fatherless, and widows. They thoroughly examine legal cases against needy people to see if there is a weakness in the evidence whether they know the victims or not. When they find injustice, they risk trouble with the poor's powerful oppressors. They stand up against them and deliver their victims. The wise's image of perfection is a society filled with Jobs.

In response to the earlier published version of this chapter,[13] J. David Pleins has contended that Wisdom literature does not contain a real teaching of social justice and that the values of the Wisdom writers were the same as those of the elite that they served.[14] To reach this conclusion, he separates Proverbs from Job and does not deal with Ecclesiastes, Sirach, or the Book of Wisdom. Apparently, then, he is evaluating only early Wisdom, as it appears in Proverbs, and not the majority of the Wisdom books which are late. Pleins emphasizes that Proverbs prefers the terms *dal, rāš,* and *maḥsôr* for the poor and uses *'ebyôn* and *'ānî* little. According to him Proverbs has a less sympathetic view of the poor than other biblical books and employs terms that give that view of the needy. However, even he admits that *dal* is used frequently in various parts of the Hebrew Bible and that *rāš* and *maḥsôr* are employed occasionally elsewhere.[15] Likewise, he admits that Proverbs uses *'ebyôn* and *'ānî* a number of times.[16] These facts make his distinction of terms less convincing.

More importantly, Pleins claims that Proverbs never goes beyond charity and reaches the level of social justice. The examination above of passages like Proverbs 13:23; 22:22; 29:7, 14; 30:13-14; and 31:9 disproves this contention. Pleins also says that an awareness that institutional evils need to be addressed is a prerequisite for labeling a perspective social justice and denies that Proverbs contains this perspective. But it is present in texts like 13:23; 22:16, 22; and 30:13-14. There is concern for social justice in Proverbs and in the rest of the Wisdom literature.

## Motivation

The Wisdom literature shows a great deal of concern with the plight of the poor. It sympathetically pictures their problems in graphic detail and appeals for their rectification through charity and justice. Why do the wise have this concern? What motivates their reaction? The writings express several different sources of motivation. For one thing, they frequently mention the fear or hope of retribution (Prov 11:24-25; 28:8, 27). 22:8-9 warns that injustice results in calamity but promises that sharing bread with the poor will bring blessing. Many passages connect the thought of retribution with God (Job 31:23; Prov 22:23; Sir 4:6; 12:3; 29:12-13). Proverbs 23:10-11 insists that readers not steal the land of the fatherless because their Redeemer is powerful and will plead their case against the offender. The Redeemer here is undoubtedly Yahweh.[17] In Israelite society a redeemer was a stronger member of the family who protected the weaker. He avenged their wrongs and defended them legally. Yahweh is the defender of the deprived who will see that they get justice. Likewise, Sirach 35:13 (NRSV v. 16) says of God:

> He will not show partiality in the case of a poor man;
> and he will listen to the prayer of one who is wronged.
> (RSV)

The first line means that Yahweh will not be partial against a poor person, as the NJB and REB make clear.[18] Verses 14-17 (NRSV 17-22) verify and amplify this interpretation. They say that God heeds the prayers and tears of wronged fatherless children and widows and comes to bring them justice.

The Wisdom books also refer to other sources of motivation besides retribution. Sirach 29:9, 11 advise giving to the poor for the sake of the commandment. Since Ben Sira has integrated Wisdom with the rest of the Hebrew Bible, he is probably referring to the Torah. It called for charity to the poor in places like Deuteronomy 15:11. So one motivation for kindness to the needy is obedience to God's commands.

Another is the equality of people. Proverbs 29:13 says that Yahweh gives light to the eyes of both the poor and their oppressors. According to 22:2, Yahweh is the maker of both rich and poor. The implication is that it is folly to attack the needy for their oppressors are no better than they since God has made them both. Similarly Sirach 10:22 says that the boast of both the rich and the poor is the fear of the Lord. They are equal in their submission to God.

An additional motive appears in Proverbs 14:31 that contends that those who are kind to the poor honor their maker. Here the compelling force toward social justice is the desire to glorify God. Still another reason for such behavior is that doing it makes the doer a child of God whom God will love more than a mother (Sir 4:10). Finally, as indicated previously, Job 29:14 says that ideal people are incarnations of justice. One can hardly talk about their motivation toward justice because that quality is entirely natural to them. They are so much children of God that the only option open to them is being just, as God is just.

Although there are problems with using retribution as a motive, as we saw in chapter 3, the wise's other reasons for social justice reach increasingly lofty levels. At their best moments, the wise saw the desire to glorify God, to be God's children, and to incarnate justice as motives toward adequately helping the poor.

Like many of the parts of Scripture studied in prior chapters, Wisdom literature is an important source of thought on social justice. Although the literary forms of Wisdom often make it difficult to perceive the particular crises which the wise faced, their frequent expressions on justice show that such crises existed. As the wise faced them, they added to Israel's legacy of social-justice thought.

## Notes

1. An earlier version of this chapter appeared in the *Biblical Theology Bulletin* 12 (1982) 120–124. Permission was granted by Biblical Theology Bulletin, Inc. for republication of "Social Justice in the Wisdom Literature."

2. Hermann Gunkel, *Einleitung in die Psalmen,* 2nd ed. (Göttingen: Vandenhoeck & Ruprecht, 1966) 383; William McKane, *Prophets and Wise Men* (Naperville: Allenson, 1965) 15.

3. J. Coert Rylaarsdam, *Revelation in Jewish Wisdom Literature* (Chicago: University of Chicago, 1946) 68–71; Roland Murphy, "Assumptions and Problems in Old Testament Wisdom Research," *CBQ* 29 (1967) 412; Gerhard von Rad, *Old Testament Theology,* trans. D. Stalker (New York: Harper & Row, 1962) 1:427, 433–39.

4. F. Charles Fensham, "Widow, Orphan, and the Poor in Ancient Near Eastern Legal and Wisdom Literature," *JNES* 21 (1962) 129; O. S.

Rankin, *Israel's Wisdom Literature* (Edinburgh: Clark, 1936) 13–15; Johannes Fichtner, *Die altorientalische Weisheit in ihrer israelitisch-jüdischen Ausprägung,* BZAW 62 (Giessen: Töpelmann, 1933) 26–31.

5. Robert Gordis, "The Social Background of Wisdom Literature," *HUCA* 18 (1944) 77–118; Glendon Bryce, *A Legacy of Wisdom* (Lewisburg: Bucknell University, 1979) 150–51; J. David Pleins, "Poverty in the Social World of the Wise," *JSOT* 37 (1987) 62; Nili Shupak, "The 'Sitz im Leben' of the Book of Proverbs in the Light of a Comparison of Biblical and Egyptian Wisdom Literature," *RB* 94 (1987) 118; Leo Perdue, "Cosmology and the Social Order in the Wisdom Tradition," *The Sage in Israel and the Ancient Near East,* ed. John Gammie and Leo Perdue (Winona Lake: Eisenbrauns, 1990) 476.

6. John Snaith, *Ecclesiasticus,* CBC (Cambridge: Cambridge University, 1974) 74; Thomas Weber, "Sirach," *JBC* 1:546.

7. William McKane, *Proverbs: A New Approach,* OTL (Philadelphia: Westminster, 1970) 435; Berend Gemser, *Sprüche Salomos,* Handbuch zum alten Testament 16, 2nd ed. (Tübingen: Mohr, 1963) 56.

8. G. Henton Davies, "Alms," *IDB* 1:87.

9. R.B.Y. Scott, *Proverbs, Ecclesiastes,* AB 18, 2nd ed. (Garden City: Doubleday, 1965) 228.

10. Robert Gordis, *Koheleth—The Man and his World,* 3rd ed. (New York: Schocken, 1968) 129–30; James Crenshaw, *Ecclesiastes, A Commentary,* OTL (Philadelphia: Westminster, 1987) 106.

11. E.g., NRSV; REB; NJB; McKane, *Proverbs,* 211.

12. Marvin Pope, *Job,* AB 15, 3rd ed. (Garden City: Doubleday, 1973) 213.

13. Bruce V. Malchow, "Social Justice in the Wisdom Literature," *BTB* 12 (1982) 120–24.

14. Pleins, "Poverty in the Social World."

15. J. David Pleins, "Poor, Poverty," *ABD* 5:405–7.

16. Pleins, "Poverty in the Social World," 63–65.

17. McKane, *Proverbs,* 380.

18. Patrick Skehan and Alexander Di Lella, *The Wisdom of Ben Sira,* AB 39 (New York: Doubleday, 1987) 419.

# Conclusion

We have completed our examination of the Hebrew Bible's statements on social justice. What have we learned from it about integrating the thoughts of non-Christians about this topic with our own Christian ideas? What model has Israel provided through the manner in which it combined its concepts with those of its non-Yahwistic neighbors?

Israel utilized prior Near Eastern thought about social justice in three ways. First, Israel merely accepted its neighbors' ideas as they were. It saw that others had valid insights and adopted them without change. For example, Israel accepted its neighbors' belief that justice was the responsibility of all of its citizens and especially of the ruler. It agreed that the special objects of social concern were the poor, widows, fatherless children, and sojourners. Also, parts of the Israelite law codes and Wisdom writings simply adopted Near Eastern injunctions on just judgment of the weak, lack of partiality in lawsuits, refraining from bribery, just weights, not moving landmarks, and charity to the poor.

Second, at times Israel made simple adaptations of Near Eastern teachings so that they applied to its own situation. Israel found specific ways to utilize more general injunctions. An example here is its adaptation of the Instruction of Amenemope's command to reduce the size of the poor's debts. Israel did this through its often repeated prohibition on charging interest on loans and through Deuteronomy's law on dissolving debts in the Sabbath Year. Also, Israel applied the frequent Near Eastern call for charity by laws on leaving gleanings in the field for the poor, letting them eat what grew in the Sabbath Year, and giving the annual tithe to them every third year. In addition, Ben Sira applied the command for charity through his liberal instruction on loans and surety.

Third, Israel transformed Near Eastern ideas when applying them to its own situation. As we have seen, transformation took place when Israel faced new justice crises. The crises motivated Israel to find new and more striking ways to call for justice. The most obvious instances occur in the prophets. They speak of some of the same problems as Near Eastern writings, such as just measure, unfair trials, bribery, and seizing the property of the poor. However, because of the extreme situations of injustice that they face, they do so with a sense of fervor and indignation not found in the previous literature. Also, Jeremiah retrieves the old idea of the just ruler but makes it a more living concept when applying it to unjust Jehoiakim.

In addition, while transforming the biblical authors break new ground and talk about justice concepts not found in previous writings because crises move them to do so. The prophets are irate over new atrocities like enslaving and killing the poor, and the extremity of the current oppression leads them to proclaim the hope for a future just age. The law givers visualize a Jubilee Year when the rich will be compelled to equalize some of their wealth with the poor. Oppression causes the psalmists to reach new heights in their image of a God who delivers and helps the deprived. And the author of Job 29 creates a sublime portrait of people who are the incarnation of justice.

Israel's three methods of accepting, adapting, and transforming are useful in our integration of non-Christian thought with our own. At times adherents of other world religions and non-religious people will create new concepts in relation to social justice that have not been part of the Christian heritage. If we evaluate them and find them useful and compatible with our theology, we can simply add them to our tradition without change. Second, when working on justice issues with these other people, there will be times when we can adapt their thought. Either we can make changes in it to apply it to a particular context that we face as Christians, or we can contribute our experience while we work together with the others on an issue, and all of us can make appropriate changes jointly. Finally, in those situations of common effort there will be moments of transformation. All of us will face new crises of injustice together, and the response that we make to them will be a transformation of all of our traditions. Ancient Israelites and Christians have always transformed their traditions in reaction to new crises. What is new is that Christians are now working jointly with other people to face justice crises and so will achieve new thought and action together with them.

Social injustice is an immense and world-wide problem. If Christians are to be true to their own tradition and ethically responsible, they must take part in the struggle against it. They will be much more effective in doing this if they join forces with other concerned people. The Hebrew Bible's approaches of acceptance, adaptation, and transformation can be of use to Christians in carrying out this common action. They will find themselves fighting injustice with what is new and what is old.

# Bibliography

Achtemeier, E. R. "Righteousness in the OT." *IDB*, vol. 4, 80–85.

Anderson, A. A. *The Book of Psalms.* Vol. 2. New Century Bible. London: Oliphants, 1972.

Anderson, Bernhard. *The Eighth Century Prophets.* Proclamation Commentaries. Philadelphia: Fortress, 1978.

Bammel, Ernst *"Ptōchos."* *TDNT*, vol. 6, 885–915.

Barrois, G. "Debt, Debtor." *IDB*, vol. 1, 809–10.

Birch, Bruce. *Let Justice Roll Down.* Louisville: Westminster, 1991.

Blenkinsopp, Joseph. *Ezra-Nehemiah, A Commentary.* OTL. Philadelphia: Westminster, 1988.

———. *A History of Prophecy in Israel.* Philadelphia: Westminster, 1983.

Boecker, Hans. *Law and the Administration of Justice in the Old Testament and Ancient East.* Trans. Jeremy Moiser. Minneapolis: Augsburg, 1980.

Bright, John. *A History of Israel.* 3rd ed. Philadelphia: Westminster, 1981.

Brueggemann, Walter. "Psalms 9–10: A Counter to Conventional Social Reality." *The Bible and the Politics of Exegesis,* ed. David Jobling and others, 3–15. Cleveland: Pilgrim, 1991.

Brueggemann, Walter, and Hans Walter Wolff. *The Vitality of Old Testament Traditions.* 2nd ed. Atlanta: John Knox, 1982.

Bryce, Glendon. *A Legacy of Wisdom.* Lewisburg: Bucknell University, 1979.

Carmichael, Calum. *The Laws of Deuteronomy.* Ithaca: Cornell University, 1974.

Childs, Brevard. *The Book of Exodus.* OTL. Philadelphia: Westminster, 1974.

Crenshaw, James. *Ecclesiastes, A Commentary.* OTL. Philadelphia: Westminster, 1987.

Davies, G. Henton. "Alms." *IDB*, vol. 1, 87–88.

Eichrodt, Walther. *Ezekiel, A Commentary.* Trans. Cosslett Quin. OTL. Philadelphia: Westminster, 1970.

———. *Theology of the Old Testament.* Vol. 1. Trans. J. A. Baker. London: SCM Press, 1961.

Fabry, H.-J. *"Dal." TDOT*, vol. 3, 208–30.

Fensham, F. Charles. "Widow, Orphan, and the Poor in Ancient Near Eastern Legal and Wisdom Literature." *JNES* 21 (1962) 129–39.

Fichtner, Johannes. *Die altorientalische Weisheit in ihrer israelitisch-jüdischen Ausprägung.* BZAW 62. Giessen: Töpelmann, 1933.

Folk, Jerry. *Doing Theology, Doing Justice.* Minneapolis: Fortress, 1991.

Fraine, J. de. *L'aspect religieux de la royauté israélite.* Analecta Biblica 3. Rome: Pontificio Istituto Biblico, 1954.

Gemser, Berend. *Sprüche Salomos.* Handbuch zum alten Testament 16. 2nd ed. Tübingen: Mohr, 1963.

Gerstenberger, Erhard. *Wesen und Herkunft des "apodiktischen Rechts."* WMANT 20. Neukirchen: Neukirchener Verlag, 1965.

Gordis, Robert. *Koheleth—The Man and his World.* 3rd ed. New York: Schocken, 1968.

———. "The Social Background of Wisdom Literature." *HUCA* 18 (1944) 77–118.

Gottwald, Norman. *The Hebrew Bible—A Socio-Literary Introduction.* Philadelphia: Fortress, 1985.

———. "Social Class as an Analytic and Hermeneutical Category in Biblical Studies." *JBL* 112 (1993) 3–22.

———. *The Tribes of Yahweh.* Maryknoll: Orbis, 1979.

Gunkel, Hermann. *Einleitung in die Psalmen.* 2nd ed. Göttingen: Vandenhoeck & Ruprecht, 1966.

Guthrie, H. "Tithe." *IDB*, vol. 4, 654–55.

Habel, Norman. *The Book of Job, A Commentary.* OTL. Philadelphia: Westminster, 1985.

Havice, Harriet. "The Concern for the Widow and the Fatherless in the Ancient Near East." Ph.D. diss., Yale University, 1979.

Hertzberg, Hans. *I & II Samuel, A Commentary.* Trans. J. S. Bowden. OTL. Philadelphia: Westminster, 1964.

Hoffner, Harry. *" 'almānāh." TDOT*, vol. 1, 287–91.

Holladay, William. *Jeremiah* 1. Hermeneia. Philadelphia: Fortress, 1986.

Hoppe, Leslie. "Isaiah 58:1-12, Fasting and Idolatry." *BTB* 13 (1983) 44–47.

Kaiser, Otto. *Isaiah 1–12, A Commentary.* Trans. John Bowden. OTL. 2nd ed. Philadelphia: Westminster, 1983.

_____. *Isaiah 13–39, A Commentary.* Trans. R. A. Wilson. OTL. Philadelphia: Westminster, 1974.

Kenyon, Kathleen. *Archaeology in the Holy Land.* New York: Frederick A. Praeger, 1960.

Klein, Ralph. "The God of the Bible Confronts the Politics of Hunger." *CurTM* 17 (1990) 110–17.

_____. *1 Samuel.* Word Biblical Commentary 10. Waco: Word Books, 1983.

Koch, Klaus. *The Prophets.* 2 vols. Trans. Margaret Kohl. Philadelphia: Fortress, 1982.

Kramer, Samuel. *The Sumerians.* Chicago: University of Chicago, 1963.

Kraus, Hans-Joachim. *Psalms 1–59, A Commentary.* Trans. Hilton Oswald. Minneapolis: Augsburg, 1988.

_____. *Psalms 60–150, A Commentary.* Trans. Hilton Oswald. Minneapolis: Augsburg, 1989.

Kuschke, A. "Arm und reich im AT." *ZAW* 57 (1939) 31–57.

Lemche, N. P. *Early Israel.* VTS 37. Leiden: E. J. Brill, 1985.

McKane, William. *Prophets and Wise Men.* Naperville: Allenson, 1965.

_____. *Proverbs: A New Approach.* OTL. Philadelphia: Westminster, 1970.

McKay, J. W. "Exodus xxiii 1-3, 6-8: A Decalogue for the Administration of Justice in the City Gate." *VT* 21 (1971) 311–25.

Mafico, Temba. "Just, Justice." *ABD,* vol. 3, 1127–29.

Malchow, Bruce V. "Social Justice in the Israelite Law Codes." *Word & World* 4 (1984) 299–306.

_____. "Social Justice in the Wisdom Literature." *BTB* 12 (1982) 120–24.

Mauch, T. "Sojourner." *IDB,* vol. 4, 397–99.

Mays, James. *Amos, A Commentary.* OTL. Philadelphia: Westminster, 1969.

_____. *Micah, A Commentary.* OTL. Philadelphia: Westminster, 1976.

Miller, J. M. and John Hayes. *A History of Ancient Israel and Judah.* Philadelphia: Westminster, 1986.

Morgenstern, J. "Jubilee, Year of." *IDB,* vol. 2, 1001–2.

Mowinckel, Sigmund. *The Psalms in Israel's Worship.* Vol. 2. Trans. D. R. Ap-Thomas. Nashville: Abingdon, 1962.

Murphy, Roland. "Assumptions and Problems in Old Testament Wisdom Research." *CBQ* 29 (1967) 407–18.

Myers, Jacob. *Ezra, Nehemiah.* AB 14. Garden City: Doubleday, 1965.

Noth, Martin. *Exodus, A Commentary.* Trans. J. S. Bowden. OTL. Philadelphia: Westminster, 1962.

_____. *The History of Israel.* 2nd ed. New York: Harper & Row, 1960.

_____. *The Laws in the Pentateuch and Other Studies.* Trans. D. Ap-Thomas. Philadelphia: Fortress, 1966.

_____. *Leviticus, A Commentary.* Trans. J. E. Anderson. OTL. Rev. ed. Philadelphia: Westminster, 1977.

Pedersen, Johannes. *Israel: Its Life and Culture.* Vol. 3. Trans. Aslaug Moller. London: Oxford University, 1959.

Perdue, Leo. "Cosmology and the Social Order in the Wisdom Literature." *The Sage in Israel and the Ancient Near East,* ed. John Gammie and Leo Perdue, 457–78. Winona Lake: Eisenbrauns, 1990.

Petersen, David. *Haggai and Zechariah 1–8, A Commentary.* OTL. Philadelphia: Westminster, 1984.

Pleins, J. David. "Poor, Poverty." *ABD,* vol. 5, 402–14.

_____. "Poverty in the Social World of the Wise." *JSOT* 37 (1987) 61–78.

Pope, Marvin. *Job.* AB 15. 3rd ed. Garden City: Doubleday, 1973.

Pritchard, J., ed. *Ancient Near Eastern Texts Relating to the Old Testament.* 3rd ed. Princeton: Princeton University, 1969.

Rad, Gerhard von. *Deuteronomy, A Commentary.* Trans. Dorothea Barton. OTL. Philadelphia: Westminster, 1966.

_____. *Old Testament Theology.* 2 vols. Trans. D. Stalker. New York: Harper & Row, 1962 and 1965.

Rankin, O. S. *Israel's Wisdom Literature.* Edinburgh: Clark, 1936.

Ringgren, Helmer. *The Messiah in the Old Testament.* Studies in Biblical Theology 18. London: SCM Press, 1956.

Roberts, J.J.M. *Nahum, Habakkuk, and Zephaniah, A Commentary.* OTL. Louisville: Westminster, 1991.

Rylaarsdam, J. Coert. *Revelation in Jewish Wisdom Literature.* Chicago: University of Chicago, 1946.

Schottroff, Willy. "The Prophet Amos: A Socio-Historical Assessment of His Ministry." *God of the Lowly,* ed. Willy Schottroff and Wolfgang Stegemann and trans. Matthew O'Connell, 27–46. Maryknoll: Orbis, 1984.

Scott, R.B.Y. "The Book of Isaiah, Chapters 1–39." *The Interpreter's Bible,* vol. 5, ed. George Buttrick and others, 149–381. Nashville: Abingdon, 1956.

_____. *Proverbs, Ecclesiastes.* AB 18. 2nd ed. Garden City: Doubleday, 1965.

Selms, A. van. "Jubilee, Year of." *IDBSupp.,* 496–98.

Shupak, Nili. "The 'Sitz im Leben' of the Book of Proverbs in the Light of a Comparison of Biblical and Egyptian Wisdom Literature." *RB* 94 (1987) 98–119.

Skehan, Patrick, and Alexander Di Lella. *The Wisdom of Ben Sira.* AB 39. New York: Doubleday, 1987.

Sklba, Richard. *Pre-exilic Prophecy.* Message of Biblical Spirituality 3. Collegeville: The Liturgical Press, 1990.

Snaith, John. *Ecclesiasticus.* CBC. Cambridge: Cambridge University, 1974.

Spencer, John. "Sojourner." *ABD,* vol. 6, 103–4.

Stiebing, William. *Out of the Desert?* Buffalo: Prometheus, 1989.

Thompson, Thomas. *Early History of the Israelite People.* Studies in the History of the Ancient Near East 4. New York: E. J. Brill, 1992.

Topel, L. John. *The Way to Peace.* Maryknoll: Orbis, 1979.

Vaux, Roland de. *Ancient Israel.* Trans. John McHugh. New York: McGraw-Hill, 1961.

Waldow, H. Eberhard von. "Social Responsibility and Social Structure in Early Israel." *CBQ* 32 (1970) 182–204.

Ward, J. M. "Isaiah." *IDBSupp.,* 456–61 .

Weber, Thomas. "Sirach." *JBC,* vol. 1, 541–55.

Weinfeld, Moshe. *Deuteronomy 1–11.* AB 5. New York: Doubleday, 1991.

Weir, J. Emmette. "The Poor are Powerless: A Response to R. J. Coggins." *Exp Tim* 100 (1988 ) 13–15.

Westermann, Claus. *Creation.* Trans. John Scullion. Philadelphia: Fortress, 1974.

_____. *Isaiah 40–66, A Commentary.* Trans. David Stalker. OTL. Philadelphia: Westminster, 1969.

Wilson, John. *The Culture of Ancient Egypt.* Chicago: University of Chicago, 1951.

Wilson, Robert. *Prophecy and Society in Ancient Israel.* Philadelphia: Fortress, 1980.

Wolf, C. U. "Poor." *IDB,* vol. 3, 843–44.

Wolff, Hans Walter. *Joel and Amos.* Trans. W. Janzen, S. McBride, and C. Muenchow. Hermeneia. Philadelphia: Fortress, 1977.

_____. *Micah, A Commentary.* Trans. Gary Stansell. Minneapolis: Augsburg, 1990.